GRAFTED IN

GRAFTED IN

LEADING YOUR ORPHAN HEART TO THE SPIRIT OF ADOPTION

MICHELLE WUESTHOFF

HEART
&
Sea
PRESS

GRAFTED IN

Trade Paperback ISBN: 978-0-692-09972-8
eBook ISBN: 978-0-692-13688-1

Copyright © 2018 by Michelle Wuesthoff

Cover Design by OK-E-KO
Layout: Roseanna White Designs
Publisher Imprint Design created by Freepik

Edited by Janna Nysewander
Author Photo by Kerby Gernander
Published in the United States by Heart&Sea Press, www.heartandseapress.com

Library of Congress Control Number: 2018907145

Printed in the United States of America

2018

Wrought from Michelle's own orphan-heart experiences, *Grafted In* guides those of us who feel disconnected from the Fathering heart of God on an important journey. With this book, you will clearly identify your need and find the path to become grafted in as a true son or daughter of the Father. *Grafted In* is everything I hoped it would be—and so much more.

Anna Le Baron, author of *The Polygamist's Daughter*

Biblically sound and inspiring, *Grafted In* by Michelle Wuesthoff will empower you to see your own identity and worth in light of God's powerful plan. You are not abandoned. God has beautifully adopted you into his forever family. The implications of this truth will positively affect every aspect of your life!

Mary DeMuth, author of *The Seven Deadly Friendships*

Grafted In is full of healing power for those secret, painful places we seldom acknowledge or reveal. It's as if God reached through Michelle's words to my tired soul and breathed the Spirit back into me. Whether you are in the midst of a painful situation or in recovery from one, this book will disciple with gentle, loving authority. Transparent, honest and humble—thank you, Michelle Wuesthoff, for sharing your mighty God story with us.

Kim de Blecourt,
author of *I Call You Mine* and *Until We All Come Home*

Michelle has captured with grace, beauty, and kindness her journey of learning to receive for herself what she desires to pass on to others. Grafted In is not a plea to expand the size of your family; it is an invitation to find yourself at home in the expanse of God's heart as Father, and God's Kingdom as Family.

Daniel Jackson, pastor at Southland Christian Church
and host of the *Ordinary Faith Podcast*

Michelle Wuesthoff has done the Body of Christ a great service. She blends her powerful testimony with biblical insight, scientific understanding, and wisdom from others. She shows the way for us to follow her in the path to adoption. Even if you read this book to help someone else, you will be touched and grow in freedom yourself. *Grafted In* will help many to move from living as orphans to enjoying the loving embrace of Father God. We welcome and celebrate this valuable book!

Mark and Jane Burlinson,

Lead Pastors, Catch the Fire Myrtle Beach

We all have unhealthy ways of dealing with our thoughts and feelings that something is wrong with us, and that somehow, we just don't fit in. "Mother of Nations," Michelle Wuesthoff, exposes the coping techniques we utilize through sharing her journey of parenting four internationally adopted children. Honest and vulnerable, and woven throughout the book, is her own process of bringing her orphaned heart to a place of wholeness. *Grafted In* is packed with wisdom and insight—take this journey, you will be so grateful.

Bob and Lore Switzer,

Family Life Pastors at Faith Worship Center

Grafted In is a timely and necessary read. We all feel misplaced; some for a moment, others struggle a lifetime. The gnawing awareness of 'not fitting in' can overwhelm our hearts, yet we were made for more. Michelle shares her journey from abandoned to entwined and teaches us how to embrace the power of God's purposeful placement into His family. This book is one you'll internalize then pass on to those who need to know that they belong.

Luann Prater, Executive Director of Encouragement Café,

and on-air personality at JoyFM

For Jody

He will not disappoint.

TABLE OF CONTENTS

PROLOGUE

As I lay sobbing and crumpled in the bushes outside our home, I knew I had reached the point of no return. There was nothing left of me—only a black hole of despair and hopelessness, snuffing out the smoldering wick my life had become. Having endured one loss after another in a very short span of time, I was unable to withstand this last one. My existence, the very light and life of my soul, was tied into each of these relationships, and with every loss, part of me died. All I wanted now was to physically go where my heart had already gone.

How does a person arrive at this point? Someone who professes to love God, their spouse, and their children? Though the paths we've taken may differ, each of us faced with those questions has a similar starting point: We don't know who we are or to whom we belong. It's a crisis of identity, ill formed from the beginning and developed in all the wrong places.

In my case, there really was no going back. I had two choices before me: First, do I choose death or life? Second, do I stay here at rock bottom, or do I find the way up and out? A day spent in the psychiatric wing of the ER helped to clarify those decisions. But even so, neither was an easy one or even a one-time choice. I had to choose both life and wholeness again and again in order to heal and move forward.

And so began the arduous process of rebuilding my identity from the ground up. As a Christian, I knew that the only way to do that was to completely dismantle the foundation I had built my identity upon and reconstruct it properly with God the Father in His rightful place. The problem was, I didn't really understand who the Father was or how to give Him that place. Exhausted and desperate, I asked Him to show me what I needed to know. His answer came in the directive for me to begin writing, and then He would speak.

And speak He did.

The following is both a true story and a prophetic one for me and for you. Through more than twenty years of parenting our four adopted children, I have gained unique insight into how fatherlessness and being an orphan affects every part of a person's identity. I understand the orphan heart very well—I just didn't recognize that I had one, too, until the Father showed me. And He showed me (as only He can do), step by step, how to bring my heart to Him and let Him love me back to life, define me, and refine me into the child He destined me to be. Even more, He showed me how to embrace my adoption and begin to thrive as a fully-loved and accepted child—one who has been *grafted in* by a loving Father. As you read this book, I pray you will allow Him to speak to your orphan heart, too, and lead it back home to Him, the Spirit of Adoption.

The Orphan

Bedraggled and bereft I wander, scraping the scorched earth beneath me
with lead-heavy feet.
Body ravaged by a prolonged hunger and thirst, my mind is too numb to fashion
a plan or scheme to meet my own needs anymore.
So long have I fought for survival that I have forgotten how to ask for help;
though still I press on—for what, I do not know.
Until by chance I meet a stranger on the road.
He waits for my approach.

He is clean and radiant.
Me? I cannot tell the difference between my outer filth and my inner defilement.
I want to retreat, but I cannot turn away from his gaze,
for the love in his eyes penetrates
the indifference in mine.
It stirs up the longing I've worked so hard to suppress, and before I know it,
I am standing there, weeping,
offering him my tin-cup heart.

CHAPTER 1

The Orphan Heart

I will not leave you as orphans [comfortless, desolate, bereaved, forlorn, helpless]; I will come [back] to you.

—John 14:18 AMPC

We were all born with an orphan heart. Every last one of us, to some degree or other, has come into this world and lived our lives from a place of abandonment, rejection, and isolation. For some of us, our outward experiences have only reinforced our inner orphan-ness, but even those of us who were welcomed and raised in a loving family have known the hunger pangs of unfulfilled needs and a deep loneliness that cannot be soothed or alleviated. This orphan status, this human condition, originated in the garden at the fall, when our first parents chose self-sufficiency over belonging and resting in the complete care of the Father.

SEVERED FAMILY TIES

From the moment they were created, Adam and Eve received everything they needed for life—even the very breath in their lungs—from their Father. Theirs was a perfect relationship in every way. God not only provided for them but also shared deep, intimate communion with them each day. It was a spirit-to-spirit connection. I'm sure the Lord delighted in their company, teaching and imparting to them all they would need to know. He did not hover over them like an overprotective parent, but gave them time to explore and learn on their own. They needed to learn how to rely on their relationship with Him and to trust and be obedient even when He was not physically present. One day, seeing an opportune moment, Satan (the original orphan) approached the couple disguised as a serpent. In the third chapter of Genesis, we read how the serpent sows doubt and mistrust in the Father's goodness into the hearts of Adam and Eve, asking them, "Did God really say, 'You must not eat from any tree in the garden'?" In this, he was suggesting that God was not only lying to them when He told them they will die if they ate from it, but that He was also withholding something good from them—wisdom—that they could get for themselves. Ironically, they then went on to make the most *unwise* choice they could have made. Their decision to eat from the Tree of Knowledge of Good and Evil was a choice of self-sufficiency, to go it alone, in order to meet their own needs and desires. And their punishment from the Lord was to receive exactly what they had chosen: independence from God, a severing of family bonds. They were banished from Eden, their home, their place of belonging and complete provision. Now they were "free" to make their own way and provide for their own needs with hearts corrupted by deceit, doubt, and mistrust.

It is significant that once Adam and Eve ate the forbidden fruit and their eyes were opened to the knowledge of good and evil, their first reaction was shame, followed by fear. Our newly orphaned parents were experiencing the first devastating symptoms of an orphan heart. At that moment, these emotions became two of the foundational conditions, or "chambers," that would govern the orphan heart and would be passed down through all the generations that followed them. Out of these two chambers (and a couple more we will get to later) flow a host of sin-sick afflictions such as

- rejection
- abandonment
- loneliness
- emptiness
- greed
- poor attachment
- over attachment
- addiction
- hard-heartedness
- independence
- indifference
- isolation
- insecurity
- helplessness
- disappointment
- hopelessness

Most of us can easily think of other symptoms to add to this list, but regardless of how they manifest in our lives, our orphan hearts operate from a place of disconnectedness, independence, and the lack of deep understanding that we belong to a Father who loves His children and wants desperately for us to find our home in Him.

Where Your Identity Is, There Your Heart Will Be Also

Naturally, how we view ourselves—as an orphan or as a true son or daughter of Father God—is a matter of identity. And it's not just a *part* of our identity, but the core of it, the foundation upon which all the other facets of our identity is built. Depending on our personal history and where we stand in our relationship with God, we may know intellectually that we are a son or daughter. We may even be able to speak that out loud and believe it at a surface level. But often in the deepest places, in our spirits, we identify with the orphan. The orphan identity, the orphan heart, the orphan spirit—however you want to label it—will inform and affect every aspect of what we think and do. It will manifest itself in a variety of traits like those I've mentioned. It will dictate how you see and respond to different circumstances, it can determine the particular path you take in life, and it will most certainly affect all aspects of your faith. But what does the orphan heart look like in action? Probably one of the best scriptural examples of those operating with orphan hearts can be found in the parable of the prodigal son, as told by Jesus:

> And he said, "There was a man who had two sons. And the younger of them said to his father, 'Father, give me the share of property that is coming to me.' And he

divided his property between them. Not many days later, the younger son gathered all he had and took a journey into a far country, and there he squandered his property in reckless living. And when he had spent everything, a severe famine arose in that country, and he began to be in need. So he went and hired himself out to one of the citizens of that country, who sent him into his fields to feed pigs. And he was longing to be fed with the pods that the pigs ate, and no one gave him anything.

"But when he came to himself, he said, 'How many of my father's hired servants have more than enough bread, but I perish here with hunger! I will arise and go to my father, and I will say to him, "Father, I have sinned against heaven and before you. I am no longer worthy to be called your son. Treat me as one of your hired servants."' And he arose and came to his father. But while he was still a long way off, his father saw him and felt compassion, and ran and embraced him and kissed him. And the son said to him, 'Father, I have sinned against heaven and before you. I am no longer worthy to be called your son.' But the father said to his servants, 'Bring quickly the best robe, and put it on him, and put a ring on his hand, and shoes on his feet. And bring the fattened calf and kill it, and let us eat and celebrate. For this my son was dead, and is alive again; he was lost, and is found.' And they began to celebrate.

"Now his older son was in the field, and as he came and drew near to the house, he heard music and dancing. And he called one of the servants and asked what these things meant. And he said to him, 'Your brother has come, and your father has killed the fattened calf, because he has received him back safe and sound.' But he was angry and refused to go in. His father came out and entreated him, but he answered his father, 'Look, these many years I have served you, and I never disobeyed your command, yet you never gave me a young goat, that I might celebrate with my friends. But when this son of yours came, who has devoured your property with prostitutes, you killed the fattened calf for him!' And he said to him, 'Son, you are always with me, and all that is mine is yours. It was fitting to celebrate and be glad, for this your brother was dead, and is alive; he was lost, and is found.'"

—Luke 15:11–32

First, let's look at the younger son, who is probably a bit more recognizable as someone possessing an orphan heart. Like his brother, he is the son of a wealthy father who owns an estate, has a sizable inheritance to leave to his sons, and has servants in his house. We aren't told why, but the younger son is clearly dissatisfied with his life under his father's roof and authority, and he asks for his inheritance up front (which, in that time and culture, was essentially wishing his father dead) in order to strike out on his own, to live life the way he wanted to, and to make his own choices. Like Adam, he chooses self-sufficiency and independence over all that comes with his birthright. Implied in his choice to leave home is the hardening of his heart against his family, and a perceived disconnect between his father and himself. It's a denial of the relationship and a lack of understanding and confidence in knowing who he is. People don't need to go out and "find themselves" when they already know who they are. With that in mind, we can see the younger son is functionally an orphan before he ever leaves home. It's not for lack of love and provision—this is, after all, the son of *the Father* that Jesus is talking about in the parable. But the enemy of our souls will sow seeds of doubt, discontent, restlessness, fear, and whatever he thinks might unsettle us and erode our sense of true identity. There are, of course, always plenty of real-world experiences to draw upon that can reinforce that erosion. The younger son may have had thousands of such experiences to prove his assumption that life on his own would be better. And so, turning his back on everything he should have known but didn't, he leaves home for a distant country. In his book *The Return of the Prodigal Son*, Henri J. M. Nouwen describes the inner spiritual reality of this choice:

> Leaving home is, then, much more than an historical event bound to time and place. It is a denial of the spiritual reality that I belong to God with every part of my being, that God holds me safe in an eternal embrace, that I am indeed carved in the palms of God's hands and hidden in their shadows. Leaving home means ignoring the truth that God has 'fashioned me in secret, moulded me in the depths of the earth and knitted me together in my mother's womb.' Leaving home is living as though I do not yet have a home and must look far and wide to find one.[1]

We can see how the prodigal's plan to run his own life works out. Not surprisingly, he squanders his inheritance (which really began in his heart while he was still at home) and he ends up penniless, starving, and enslaved, living the lifestyle of the stereotypical orphan. What is poignant, though, is that when he remembers his father and decides to return home, it is not a sudden realization of his sonship. His mind and heart have clearly not changed significantly. For "when he came to himself" (returning to his usual way of thinking), he ultimately decides to renounce his sonship altogether and live as a servant in order to earn food, provision, and a place within his father's house. Not only does the younger son not know who *he* is, he obviously doesn't know who his father is either! More on that in chapter 2.

Surprisingly, even the elder son operates with an orphan's heart. Upon hearing that his brother is back home and their father is throwing a party for him, the "good and responsible" brother's first reactions are of anger, bitterness, and resentment. These reactions flow from a heart and spirit corrupted by insecurity, jealousy, and self-righteousness; wounded by the deeply cultivated perception that he was not good enough or loved enough by his father to be worthy of the celebration his brother was getting. Like his younger brother, he felt he had earned what he had received from his father through his service and obedience. It is also implied that he thought he earned more than he had actually received. He thought he knew what being a true son was, but now his understanding was being turned upside down as he watched his father's reaction to his disobedient brother's return. The elder brother also does not know who his father is or recognize his true position in his father's life.

THE FOUR CHAMBERS OF AN ORPHAN HEART: SOUL LONELINESS, RESTLESS WANDERING, SHAME, AND FEAR

It is perhaps easier to realize that you have lived life as an orphan when you've found yourself lost or alone in a distant country, made colossal mistakes, or have been powerless to help yourself out of a difficult situation. But what if you are hardworking and successful and seemingly have your life together—could you still be living with an orphan's heart? I would answer an emphatic *yes!* Most times I would say I fit the part of the elder brother better than that of the younger, "prodigal" one. However, I can also say from my own experience that outward appearances of virtue and success frequently belie the inner turmoil and restlessness that rages under the surface, stemming from an identity not rooted in the love of God or His Fatherhood over us. Whether you are more like the younger brother or the older one, or perhaps a little like each of them at different times in your life, chances are that at some point you have lived your life as a spiritual orphan. So, let's look at the foundational conditions, or "four chambers," of the orphan heart:

SOUL LONELINESS

God, but life is loneliness, despite all the opiates, despite the shrill tinsel gaiety of "parties" with no purpose, despite the false grinning faces we all wear. And when at last you find someone to whom you feel you can pour out your soul, you stop in shock at the words you utter — they are so rusty, so ugly, so meaningless and feeble from being kept in the small cramped dark inside you so long. Yes, there is joy, fulfillment and companionship — but the loneliness of the soul in its appalling self-consciousness is horrible and overpowering.

—Sylvia Plath[2]

I will never forget the night, several years ago, when it was my turn to lead a young women's Bible study that I co-led with a friend. I thought it would be interesting and meaningful to discuss a topic relevant to all of us and explore what God said about it in His Word. After our opening prayer, I looked out on the circle of smiling, expectant faces of my friends and said, "Tonight I want to talk about loneliness." Immediately several women burst into tears. What is it about loneliness? That clawing, nagging, aching emptiness we carry that is so present and constant, that no matter how deeply we try to bury or suppress it, the mere mention of it can dissolve us on the spot? I'm convinced it is one of the primary conditions of the orphan heart. Let me explain why. We were created by a triune God; three persons (Father, Son, and Holy Spirit) who are in perfect, inseparable communion with one another. Perfectly satisfied and sustained within the Godhead, there was no need for additional relationship, but it pleased Him greatly to create human beings to have relationship with: "Then God said, 'Let us make man in our image, after our likeness'" (Genesis 1:26). We were made in the image and likeness of a God who embodies deep relationship at His core. Think about that. We are made in the image of the One who is Three—the One who is family, friend, and community all within Himself. We were created to share in that communion so that our whole being (body, mind, soul, and spirit) would function within and be perfectly satisfied by direct, intimate relationship with our Creator. Heartbeats and breathing in sync, whispers from spirit to spirit unhindered by outside forces, love flowing freely through open, unbroken channels to and from the Father … that kind of communion. Isn't the thought of it deeply satisfying? It's what we were made like and it's what we were made for! Adam and Eve enjoyed this kind of relationship with God until they were persuaded by the serpent to believe that something better was out there that God wasn't giving them. I've often thought it was curious that the serpent spoke to them. There is no other mention in Genesis of animals being able to speak, and I wonder if Adam and Eve became fascinated and enticed by the serpent because of that—by speaking to them, the serpent was introducing and offering to them a kind of counterfeit relationship. When their fascination made room for doubt and mistrust, Satan had them exactly where he wanted them. Consequently, the previously unbroken channel of relationship with God was cut. This spiritual separation, along with actual physical death, is what God was warning them about when He told them that if they ate of the tree, "in the day that you eat of it you shall surely die" (Genesis 2:17b). They did not physically die the day they ate it; in fact, they lived for hundreds of years afterward, about which I'm sure Satan was happy to remind them. However, that very day, the spirit-to-spirit connection to God they were born with died a permanent death. And with that death came an enormous void, a soul loneliness we were never intended to have.

RESTLESS WANDERING

"My people have been lost sheep. Their shepherds have allowed them to go astray. They have wandered around in the mountains. They have roamed from one mountain and hill to another. They have forgotten their resting place."

—Jeremiah 50:6 NET

In his poem contained in *The Fellowship of the Ring*, J.R.R. Tolkien famously wrote, "Not all who wander are lost."[3] So beautifully said and very true; not all are, especially not the One to whom Tolkien is referring. But implied in that quote is the truth that most who are wandering around are, in fact, lost—restless and searching for something they cannot find where they are. We've all been there, probably multiple times throughout our lives in a variety of circumstances. Many of us, however, suffer with this restless wandering as a permanent inner condition. It's a state of spiritual "homelessness," making us feel we don't belong anywhere or to anyone. Jack Frost, former fishing boat captain and founder of Shiloh Place Ministries, was one of the first to teach and write about the orphan spirit. In his book *Spiritual Slavery to Spiritual Sonship*, Jack talks about the same condition of homelessness:

> Home is the place where you can go and hear the voice of your Father say, "No matter what anybody else says, you are the child I love and on whom My favor rests." Home is where you constantly hear the voice of God speaking His affirmation over you, His love over you, and His forgiveness, compassion, and grace over you. Without this deep, experiential knowledge and understanding of Father's love and that you have a home in Him, it becomes so easy to live your life as if you don't have a home....[4]

The kind of home he speaks of is the resting place where our soul and spirit can dwell in peace. However, the restless wandering of the orphan heart dictates that no matter what we do or where we are, no matter how good life looks on the outside, we cannot escape the unsettledness on the inside, the lack of inner peace and contentment, and the feeling that there must be something more, better, or different elsewhere that will alleviate our quiet angst. I'm sure this was the experience that Adam and Eve had once they were cast out of the garden, and the turmoil that must have been eating at the Prodigal Son, prompting him to leave home. And lest we deceive ourselves (or be deceived), restless wandering isn't the same thing as adventure seeking or a desire to get out and pioneer some uncharted territory—you know the difference. This is the sort of restlessness that makes commitment difficult and unpleasant, focus and drive hard to sustain, and solitude or quiet too painful to bear. This restlessness drives us to aimlessly fritter away hours on the Internet or at the mall, to lose ourselves in shopping or eating, into fantasy or casual intimacy, or to a whole host of other things. It's like consuming imaginary food in an attempt to satiate a real and persistent hunger. Of course, advertising and marketing and our consumer-driven culture do nothing but encourage this fruitless pursuit. Because we do not know where and to Whom we belong, our orphan hearts allow other things to become our shepherds and lead us astray. Each enticing promise returns void, and we are left to search and wander again, like orphans without a home. Moreover, restless wandering and soul loneliness go hand in hand, reinforcing the aching emptiness each condition carries, becoming cornerstones in the foundation of the orphan heart.

Shame

Shame is a soul eating emotion.
—Carl Jung[5]

Shame is another cornerstone in the foundation of the orphan heart. You might even say it was the first stone laid in the foundation, as we revisit what happened when Adam and Eve took their first bite of fruit: "At that moment their eyes were opened, and they suddenly felt shame at their nakedness. So they sewed fig leaves together to cover themselves" (Genesis 3:7 NLT). I have always thought it was strange that their shame response was to their nakedness and not to their disobedience. However long they were living before they ate the fruit, they had always been naked—it was all they had ever known—and there was nothing inherently bad about their nakedness, since God Himself created them that way. So first of all, we can interpret that shame is an emotion born out of a distortion, a lie resulting from sin. It also points its finger away from the truth and at something else, perhaps so we fail to deal with the root cause directly. Because Adam and Eve's sin caused an immediate disruption in the spirit-to-spirit communion they had with God, shame was also the immediate consequence of that channel being cut, because shame is relational in character. It emphasizes sin's effect on self-identity.[6] As Jung so insightfully determined, it can be a "soul eating emotion." Shame, like the enemy that ushered it in, is a usurper, a liar, and an oppressor, keeping the orphan heart from experiencing the freedom, joy, and identity in Christ we were designed to have. Though it hides quietly in dark places, it speaks loudly: *You are worthless. You're a nothing—disgusting and despicable. Who do you think you are, anyway?* It makes us want to cower and hide, and it engulfs us. It is like the ultimate parasite, feeding off whatever it can latch onto, growing bigger as it consumes more, and though it may go dormant, it resurfaces with a vengeance when triggered, always aiming to keep the other chambers of the orphan heart in place and in check.

Fear

I must say a word about fear. It is life's only true opponent. Only fear can defeat life. It is a clever, treacherous adversary, how well I know. It has no decency, respects no law or convention, shows no mercy. It goes for your weakest spot, which it finds with unnerving ease. It begins in your mind, always … so you must fight hard to express it. You must fight hard to shine the light of words upon it. Because if you don't, if your fear becomes a wordless darkness that you avoid, perhaps even manage to forget, you open yourself to further attacks of fear because you never truly fought the opponent who defeated you.

—Yann Martel, *Life of Pi*[7]

The fourth chamber of the orphan heart is fear. Fear, like shame, entered on the scene at the fall, at once shackling mankind in bondage to the enemy of our souls. Also like shame, fear paralyzes, incapacitates, and makes us feel powerless over our circumstances and ourselves. Fear can mingle with or precipitate soul loneliness and restless wandering, as well, so it is a powerful component not only in the makeup of the orphan heart but also in keeping the other components active and in place. It can be difficult to fully address the loneliness and restlessness we experience if fear (or shame) is not addressed and removed. Attacks of fear can be bold and uncontainable—like panic attacks—or they can be subtle and manageable yet equally effective in holding us back from all we can be or do. Fear can reduce any of us to a childlike state—weak and vulnerable, exposed and helpless. It can also numb us or provoke us to disengage from whatever makes us feel something we don't want to feel. And what we fear, we become subject to. Fear of God is healthy in that respect, as is a rational fear of what is truly dangerous to our health and safety. Most of what we fear, however, does not fall into these categories—many fears we live with are irrational, illogical, and completely unhealthy. They cause us to feel smaller than the thing we fear. The orphan heart, therefore, becomes subject to whatever makes it feel afraid, and fear is a very cruel master.

THE FOUR CHAMBERS
of the **ORPHAN** HEART:

THE ARCHETYPES OF AN ORPHAN HEART

The makeup and content of the heart not only informs and influences our identities but also our unique personalities. Despite the uniqueness of the individual, common personality traits tend to emerge in those who live out of an orphan identity. I began to see and experience this for myself while working with orphans in Africa. Each year over a period of five years, I visited Uganda to work with children and families in a child-sponsorship program I helped establish. It was founded within the framework of an existing orphanage as a ministry and outreach to the surrounding communities. During those years, I spent time with hundreds of orphaned children and young adults. Some were orphaned due to the sickness or death of one or both parents, others to abandonment, and many were simply given over to the orphanage or another family because their parents were too poor to care for them. In every case, each child suffered tremendous loss, but how their particular trauma displayed itself was as wide and varied as the children themselves. Generally, though, their orphan personalities fell into a few different archetypes:

THE LONE-RANGING HUSTLER

The tragedy of it is that nobody sees the look of desperation on my face. Thousands and thousands of us, and we're passing each other by without a look of recognition.

—Henry Miller[8]

These orphans were fiercely independent and seemingly self-sufficient. Intelligent and creative, they actively sought the quickest, most effective ways to get their needs met. In doing so, they could be incredibly charming and persuasive or, if need be, ruthless and manipulative. Their steely eyes were constantly sizing up their environment and the people around them. They projected boldness and confidence, indifference and hard-heartedness, and though I saw many of these kids hanging out in groups, it was clear that they were just a collection of lone rangers, each one out for themselves. They were survivors, and successful ones at that.

I remember meeting a boy called Stephen on the playground during my first mission trip to Uganda. Before we knew his name, we referred to him as "Mr. Cool" because every day he wore sunglasses to the children's camp we were hosting. He had this uncanny ability to be everywhere you were while still remaining somewhat aloof. Though he couldn't have been more than twelve, he had the type of personality you might encounter at a pick-up bar—he was a smooth talker with an agenda you could spot a mile away. He was looking to score some toys or stickers or whatever trinkets we had with us, and you could feel the emptiness he carried. It was palpable.

It is not hard to imagine orphan hearts and personalities like Stephen's reflected within many people we know in our fast-paced Western society. Many of us function just like that. *It is difficult, if not impossible, to trust people. I cannot afford to be that vulnerable. Don't let anyone in too far—I must protect myself at all costs. No one will look out for me, so I must take care of number one … I will get what I deserve, for the good or for the bad. It's just my lot in life, the hand I was dealt. Make the most of today, because tomorrow is not promised.*

THE POSTER CHILD

As soon as someone accuses me or criticizes me, as soon as I am rejected, left alone, or abandoned, I find myself thinking, "Well, that proves once again that I am a nobody." ... [My dark side says,] I am no good ... I deserve to be pushed aside, forgotten, rejected, and abandoned. Self-rejection is the greatest enemy of the spiritual life because it contradicts the sacred voice that calls us the "Beloved." Being the Beloved constitutes the core truth of our existence.

— Henri J. M. Nouwen[9]

There were children I met who fit every stereotype we think of when we hear the word *orphan*. These are the types we see on late-night infomercials for sponsorship or aid programs—ones that stir up strong emotions when we see them. Their countenance and frame shouts abandonment, loss, rejection, and heartbreak. They are malnourished physically, spiritually, and emotionally; their eyes are sad and pleading. They may eagerly receive but have virtually nothing to give. They are the proverbial empty tin cup longing to be filled. Some position themselves to be seen and helped; others hide from view in despair and hopelessness. Even among the many people bustling here and there on the busy sidewalks, they are alone; they know it, and you know it when you see them. They desperately await rescue but have no real hope it will come.

One of the most heartbreaking sights I've ever seen was a little girl, not even two years old, begging on a busy sidewalk in the business district of Kampala. She sat cross-legged and motionless, tiny hands held out and cupped together. She did not make eye contact with anyone. I was abruptly cautioned by a local not to give her anything, because her mother had placed her there and was hiding out of sight somewhere nearby. We weren't supposed to reward her for using her child like that. Can you imagine growing up in an atmosphere of such desperation? Who knows what it took to get that little girl to sit still like that for so long. Though her open hands spoke a whisper of hope, her empty gaze and flat expression shouted otherwise.

Even if our own life stories are drastically different from the sad plight of this little one, some of us feel on the inside and reflect on the outside this same type of orphan personality. *I'm afraid and alone and no one will help me … I'm exhausted from fighting for survival; this life is pain and bitter disappointment. I want someone to love me, to help me, to rescue me from my circumstances and myself, but I don't really believe any of that will come or will last if it does.*

THE GOOD ORPHAN

> Being unwanted, unloved, uncared for, forgotten by everybody, I think that is a much greater hunger, a much greater poverty than the person who has nothing to eat.
>
> —Mother Teresa[10]

These children usually were the favorites of foreign visitors, which was their explicit aim. They knew how to be polite, engaging, happy, and affectionate. Quickly, they would melt your heart with their hugs, admiring gazes, and profuse *I love you*s. Some would call you "mommy" or "daddy" the first day they met you and ask for you to take them home with you. There were others that did a fair amount of hustling themselves—sometimes for stuff, but most times just for love and praise. It was easy to become fond of them but also easy to see before long that they were gaping holes you could never fill, leading you to feel uncomfortable and sad for them, and even pulled into their desperation yourself. Usually, though, these children could not keep up this level of "goodness" too long—those of us who stayed around long enough watched them become sullen and withdrawn, sinking back inside their inner loneliness-and-disappointment-filled world.

This kind of thing happens after the "honeymoon phase" when you first adopt older children, too. Initially, the kids are "on" all the time, interested and excited about everything, because it's all new and wonderful. But they learn quickly that all the stuff they thought would make them happy just can't fill their empty places or fix the broken pieces. The happy wears off and gives way to pain.

You have to wonder how many people out there fit this archetype; sometimes without real spiritual discernment, you might not recognize the pain and emptiness that lies beneath the cheerful façade. Certainly not all outwardly happy people are orphans on the inside, but many more are than we might otherwise assume. These orphans strive and struggle to please and to feel loved: *If you just love me, I promise I'll be good. You can give me the true happiness and belonging I am looking for—I just know you could! If I work hard enough at it, I know I can make you love me. Please don't leave me.*

The Cynical Opportunist

The truth is you can be orphaned again and again and
again. The truth is you will be. And the secret is, this will
hurt less and less each time until you can't feel a thing.
Trust me on this.

—Chuck Palahniuk[11]

Remmy grew up on the streets of Wakiso, abandoned by his
parents and suffering from a disfiguring skin condition. He was
taunted and teased about his appearance and, as you can imagine,
grew up feeling cast aside and worthless. He was extremely
intelligent and resourceful, however, and though he scraped and
struggled to make it happen, he learned to provide for himself.
When I first met him, Remmy was polite but as cynical as they
come. He had been hurt too much to allow himself to feel loved—
or to feel much of anything.

Orphans like Remmy have already seen it all and protect their
fragile hearts behind a hard shell of jadedness, disillusionment, and
disengagement. They are mostly even-keeled, not given to become
emotional or emotionally involved with anyone or anything. They
are pleasant enough conversationally as long as it's surface talk,
but start treading on deeper ground with them and they grow
uncomfortable and cynical about life, about relationships, and
about hope. They don't hustle for what they need but take what
comes when it's offered to them. "Take what you can get while
you can get it" would be their motto. There is a quiet sadness
about them, a dim light behind their eyes and their smile. If there
is hope for a better tomorrow, they'll believe it when they see it.

But probably not. We've all met people like this and probably attributed what we see and hear to a bad attitude or a chip on the shoulder, rather than a deeply wounded heart that is just trying to self-protect. *Whatever. I'm used to it.*

These archetypes are obviously generalizations of character and personality. Although there are invariably some individuals that fit one type perfectly, most people can recognize a combination of qualities and behaviors that fit their unique orphan makeup. Before outlining the path to healing, it has been important for me to begin by answering these questions: What is an orphan heart? Where did it come from and why does it exist? What does it look like and how does it operate? Now that I've answered those questions, I pose this one to you: Does any of this sound at all like *you*?

Cry of the Heart

Call me your own.
Look me in the eyes and tell me, knowing everything you do,
that you would still choose me.
Know me, hear me, love me.
Take me in to the secret places of your heart and let me stay there.
Let the kindness of your gaze and the gentleness of your spirit
minister the sweet familiarity of home to my every place of longing,
and displace the burden of its weight.
Tell me I belong and that you delight in me;
fill my troubled thoughts with your approval and hope
until they crowd out the self-defeating mantras I recite.

Allow me to be your friend, but be my father, my protector, my guide.
Be the object of my love and desire, more perfect than any lover;
instill purity into my passion, holiness into my infatuation.
Grow my love for you, for you are worthy of it beyond anyone or anything
I have ever known.
Satisfy my soul, but keep me hungry and thirsty for more of you.

Great and Majestic is the name and renown of my King, my Friend,
Father, Lover, and Master.
Call to me and I will answer!
Let me stay with you forever.

CHAPTER 2

The Father's Heart

See what great love the Father has lavished on us, that we should be called children of God! And that is what we are!

—1 John 3:1 NIV

Now that we know where we are coming from, we need to know where we are going. *Really* know! If you are a long-time believer like I am, don't be tempted to gloss over the retelling of God's great love and His Father's heart, even if you have heard or read about it thousands of times. Sometimes I find myself doing that, particularly if they are familiar verses. But the truth is—*especially* if you have been living your whole life with an orphan heart—you probably don't know or understand the love of God as well or as deeply as you think you do. So, close your eyes for a moment and ask the Lord to breathe a new, fresh revelation of His love into your heart. Ask Him to prepare your mind to receive and meditate on it, that He would remove any obstacles in the way, or show you the obstacles that He would have you remove. Once you've done that, read on.

LAVISH LOVE

One of the best, most incredible things about the Word of God is that it is living and active and that He is always in the process of making things new (Hebrews 4:12; Revelation 21:5). That means we can never exhaust our knowledge and application of His Word—never! Every reading can hold a new, fresh revelation of His love, His goodness, His character, or anything else He wants to speak about to us. We can never know enough about or receive too much of His love. All the books ever written (including the Bible) cannot contain or quantify the magnitude of His love. Once, during a visit to the beach, the Lord spoke these words in my spirit, words I will never forget:

> *See that ocean you love so much? Think of how vast it is, how deep, how wide. Think of the volumes it can contain! Think of how the horizon stretches out to infinity in your sight. I am telling you, all of that cannot contain my love for you. It is bigger. It is deeper. It is wider. And it has no end.*

His great, lavish love. If only we could ponder that until we truly understand it! I discovered something that surprised and amazed me when I looked up the definition of *lavish*. I wanted to write more about its meaning in order to elaborate on it and drive it home, and this is what I discovered. *Lavish* means "using or giving in great amounts" and … to my amazement … "prodigal"! Hold on—like the Prodigal Son? I had always thought *prodigal* meant something akin to "wayward," so I looked up its definition and found this: "wastefully or recklessly extravagant." Think about that. It makes perfect sense applied to the Prodigal Son, who took his extravagant inheritance and squandered it recklessly. Now contrast that to his father, *the Prodigal Father*, who spends His extravagant love recklessly on us! He is the perfectly fitting antidote to our hopelessly sinful condition. His love, flowing from His fatherly heart, is the cure for the orphan heart, lavished recklessly on us through our adoption.

THE PRODIGAL FATHER

Earlier in chapter 1, I said that not only did the two sons not know who they really were, they did not know who their father was, either. Let's take a look now at the heart of the Father, as we see it displayed in these verses of the parable:

The father divided his estate between the two sons, and he let the younger son go.

- All that the father has he gives to his children; he holds nothing back.

- Presumably, the two sons have always had the same kinds of temperaments: the older, hardworking and responsible; the younger, impatient, impulsive, and ungrateful. Their inheritance is divided equally between them, without favoritism given to the better-behaved son. That's because their inheritance is not given to them based on the sons' worthiness of it, but on the love and generosity of the father.

- The father allows the younger son freedom to choose what he wants, even when that puts the inheritance at stake. He wants children who choose to love him freely; he will not force them into relationship.

"How many of my father's servants have more than enough bread?"

- The father's house is a house of abundance; there is always more than enough.

- All in the father's house are provided for generously, not just the sons.

"I will arise and go to my father …"

- The Prodigal Son trusts in his father's kindness and goodness, and knows him to be just and reasonable, at least enough to know he can return to him.

- The son understands repentance will arouse his father's compassion.

"But while he was still a long way off, his father saw him and felt compassion, and ran and embraced him and kissed him."

- How is the father able to see his son while he was still a long way off? *He was watching for him!* The father never gave up hope that his son would return.

- The father felt compassion for his son—for the state he was in, for his failings, for his desperation. And his compassion far outweighed his disappointment or any other (justified) offense he might have held against his son.

The father *ran* to him. He did not wait for his son to approach him; he chose the more vulnerable posture. I read somewhere once that in Jesus' day, it would have been highly undignified for a wealthy man of the father's stature to run at all, and even more so to lift his robe and bare his ankles as he would have needed to do in order to run. The father was so caught up in love for his son, he did not care about how he looked to others!

- He embraced his son and kissed him. The father cannot contain his great love or his affection for his son. This is not merely a "welcome home" hug, but an impassioned, heartbroken-turned-joyous embrace. I can picture the son completely enveloped in the folds of his father's robe. The father's love quite literally covering a multitude of his sins.

The father gave him new clothes, a ring, and new shoes.

- This was about more than just meeting the son's needs, although he does indeed do that. Throughout the Bible, how one is clothed very often represents the state of the one wearing them (clothed in righteousness, in mourning, in forgiveness, in power, etc.). Here, the father exchanges the son's dirty garments for clean ones that he provides, which sounds a lot like forgiveness and cleansing to me. I have often pictured the father placing the robe on the son as a mantle of anointing and as an article of clothing that would make the son recognizable as one who is now set apart. The ring, an extravagant gift by nature, symbolizes dignity, power, and authority; and shoes, equipping for the walk of faith and of service.

The father is so overjoyed he throws an extravagant party.

- It would have been more than enough for the father to celebrate with a nice dinner for only his two sons and himself, but it pleased the father to share his happiness and his hospitality with others—even the servants. His heart is immensely glad, generous, and inclusive!

The father also goes out to the elder son to plead with him to join them, and reassures and comforts him.

- His joy is not complete unless all his children are in his house with him.

- His desire is for both his sons to understand their place in his heart. He also wants the older son to share in his joy, and to love his brother as the father does.

The love the Father has for His children trumps all—all offenses, all judgment, all sin. It's not that these things don't matter to Him. They do. But His lavish love gives birth to mercy, compassion, and forgiveness when what we deserve is judgment, penalty, and estrangement for our prodigal ways. As a parent, I have not had the experience of any of my children taking all we've given them and waving us off as they walk away with no intention of returning. Thank God for that. I know there are others who have experienced that heartbreak, that gut-wrenching pain of bitter grief and loss. Surely the Lord knows that pain full well and shares in their sorrow. But even if we ourselves are not actively, consciously rejecting the Father, those of us with an orphan heart actually are going the way of the prodigals.

All parents experience rejection to some degree from their children; adoptive parents experience it from theirs on a whole different level. Our adoptees, who have endured the most primary form of rejection, can become masters of rejection themselves in order to self-protect. Most of us dread and try to steel ourselves against the inevitable "You're not my real mom (or dad)!" that is bound to escape the mouths of our children at some time or another. We all know what they are getting at, but all the same, it can be so disheartening because we often work overtime trying to teach them what *real* truly means. We spend an enormous amount of time defining parent and child roles, because it is painfully clear they don't see them accurately. We want so badly for our kids to *get it*, to understand how much they are loved, how deeply they belong, how vastly we care about every little part of their lives— past, present, and future. How much more so does our Father in heaven long for that for each one of us?

But despite our desire (or the Father's) to communicate those things, it can be extremely challenging to make any headway when you are dealing with an orphan. Not that we as parents view them that way—we see them as true sons and daughters—it is the children who still see themselves through an orphan identity. And that's the parallel I'm drawing here—we are also orphans who require those roles to be defined for us, often repeatedly, and even *then* we are still slow to get it. There is an enormous chasm between the orphan heart and the Father's heart, at least from our perspective, so it is crucial to know how to bridge that gap in order to lead the orphan heart home, where it can be enveloped in the loving embrace of the Father's heart.

THE FATHER'S HEART LOOKS LIKE JESUS

If you want to know what the Father's heart looks like, all you have to do is look at Jesus. In the next chapter, we'll look at the Father's heart through the life of Jesus in more depth. The Bible says He is the "exact representation of his being." Jesus himself says, "Anyone who has seen me has seen the Father" (Hebrews 1:3; John 14:9 NIV). And this is what we see: a Father who heals every sickness He encounters; one who calls little children to Himself and blesses them, one who patiently teaches, and one who weeps for the lonely, the lost, and the hard of heart.

He calms the storm for those who are afraid, feeds those who are hungry, befriends the lepers and prostitutes and tax collectors. He shows righteous anger toward those who oppress His beloved, at demons that torment His neighbors, and at religious leaders who put their love of power and money above love for the people. He takes ordinary people and outcasts and raises them up as partners in His ministry and in the working of miracles; He does not keep what He does shrouded in mystery, but teaches them—and us— openly how to do what He does. Like a perfect father (for He is one) He comforts, bears our burdens, and lays down His very life for His children. He even gives us a new heart, exchanging ours for His own. He is goodness, and truth, and compassion, and love personified. Blessed is the Lord, our Savior, Redeemer, Friend, and *Father*!

His *Hesed* Heart

It is, of course, impossible to sum up the love of God and the heart of the Father in a single chapter of a book—or at all, for that matter. But I want to touch upon something that just might be my favorite characteristic of God, and that is His covenantal, *hesed* love. *Hesed* is a Hebrew word that has no exact English translation, but it can be described as His steadfast, loyal, faithful, unfailing love expressed through God's covenant relationship with His children. When He leads Moses and the Hebrews out of Egypt, He establishes Israel as a nation, a people set apart for Him. Time and time again He repeats His covenant promise to them: "You will be my people and I will be your God." And He reminds them why He has chosen them and what kind of God He is:

> "The LORD did not set his heart on you and choose you because you were more numerous than other nations, for you were the smallest of all nations! Rather, it was simply that the LORD loves you, and he was keeping the oath he had sworn to your ancestors. That is why the LORD rescued you with such a strong hand from your slavery and from the oppressive hand of Pharaoh, king of Egypt. Understand, therefore, that the LORD your God is indeed God. He is the faithful God who keeps his covenant for a thousand generations and lavishes his unfailing [*hesed*] love on those who love him and obey his commands."
>
> —Deuteronomy 7:7–9 NLT

The word *hesed* is used 248 times in the Old Testament, in

nearly every book. The Psalms are rich with *hesed*, translated as "mercy" in many instances but also as "lovingkindness" and "steadfast, unfailing love" in many others. It is *hesed* love that David speaks of in Psalm 23 when he says, "Surely goodness and mercy [*hesed*] shall follow me all the days of my life," and that Jeremiah speaks of in Lamentations 3:21–23:

> But this I call to mind,
> and therefore I have hope:
> The steadfast [*hesed*] love of the LORD never ceases;
> his mercies never come to an end;
> they are new every morning;
> great is your faithfulness.

One of the most beautiful expressions of the Father's *hesed* heart is found in the book of Hosea, particularly in the first three chapters. Hosea was a prophet—a contemporary of Amos, Micah, and Isaiah—during the reign of the evil king Jeroboam and a rapid succession of short-term kings after him. Israel had forsaken God, reveling in the days of material prosperity and worshiping Baal. During this era "there [was] no faithfulness or steadfast love [*hesed*], and no knowledge of God in the land" (Hosea 4:1b). The Lord commanded Hosea to marry Gomer, a prostitute (or a woman who would later prostitute herself) as a symbol of Israel's unfaithfulness to God. Every part of Gomer's life had symbolic meaning attached to it, including the naming of the children she bore: "God sows," (Hosea's biological child), "No Mercy," and "Not My People" (the children Gomer conceives out of wedlock). Despite Hosea's dedication and love for her, Gomer leaves him, chooses infidelity, and eventually needs to be purchased back by Hosea from her lover to return home—she is, in fact, the prodigal wife.

Though the Lord allows Gomer to experience the consequences of her actions, this is what He speaks of her and, therefore, of Israel:

"Therefore, behold, I will allure her,

and bring her into the wilderness *(a place of trial and testing),*
and speak tenderly to her *(to her heart).*
And there I will give her her vineyards
and make the Valley of Achor *(valley of trouble)* a door of hope.
And there she shall answer as in the days of her youth,
as at the time when she came out of the land of Egypt.

"And in that day, declares the LORD, you will call me 'My Husband,' and no longer will you call me 'My Baal' *('my owner').* For I will remove the names of the Baals from her mouth, and they shall be remembered by name no more. And I will make for them a covenant on that day with the beasts of the field, the birds of the heavens, and the creeping things of the ground. And I will abolish the bow, the sword, and war from the land, and I will make you lie down in safety. **And I will betroth you to me forever. I will betroth you to me in righteousness and in justice, in steadfast love and in mercy. I will betroth you to me in faithfulness. And you shall know the LORD.** *(This is hesed love!)*

(And of her children he says:)

"And in that day I will answer, declares the LORD,
I will answer the heavens,

and they shall answer the earth,

and the earth shall answer the grain, the wine, and the oil,

and they shall answer Jezreel *(God sows)*,

and I will sow her for myself in the land.

And I will have mercy on No Mercy,

and I will say to Not My People, 'You are my people';

and he shall say, 'You are my God.'"

—Hosea 2:14–23

This is the full redemption and restoration of Gomer and of Israel, promised by the Prodigal Father, lovesick for His children; recklessly, wastefully lavishing His extravagant love, forgiveness, mercy, and kindness on them all. Again, the verse that reads, *I will betroth you to me forever. I will betroth you to me in righteousness and in justice, in steadfast love and in mercy. I will betroth you to me in faithfulness*—that is the *hesed* heart of the Father! It means He's not giving up on you, He's not going to stop loving you, He's never letting go. When we are betrothed to Him, belong to Him, come home to Him, and abide in Him … *then we shall know the Lord!*

And this lovesick Father with His *hesed* heart, the One who waits at the door, cannot bear to let us go it alone anymore without His rescue. So He comes to us as God incarnate, in the person of Jesus. He comes to us (running, as it were) to save us, to fulfill His covenant promise to us, and to lead us home into His loving arms, where we belong.

Love Came Down

Yahweh, King of the Universe, You have humbled Yourself
and come down to me at my level;
You chose to get up from Your throne
(though in truth, Your throne is never vacant)
and sit on the floor with me in my humility, my nakedness, my shame.
You know the unspoken desires of my heart,
the things I would never dare to ask for,
the words I didn't even know I longed to hear,
and You speak them to me in my own language.
You are the LORD of all, the Almighty God, and You could very well choose
to speak to me and act however You please.
Yet You often choose what pleases me.
You are so big and so great that I cannot comprehend the magnitude
of all that You are,
yet You choose to make Yourself gentle and vulnerable to me, to my desires,
to my fragile heart.
You are the God who woos me, who pursues me,
who spoils me with extravagant displays of love; You, who are perfectly righteous
and good, care about winning my trust and my affection.
You are willing to wait for me as long as it takes,
willing to get Your spotless hands dirty on my behalf, in order to help me tear
down walls and clean up the garbage of my life;
all so I can know and experience more of Your love.
And Love is who You are, what You do; and in Love, You came.
You came as Love and came down
for me.

CHAPTER 3

Jesus Leads the Way

"My sheep hear My voice, and I know them, and they follow Me. And I give them eternal life, and they shall never perish; neither shall anyone snatch them out of My hand. My Father, who has given them to Me, is greater than all; and no one is able to snatch them out of My Father's hand. I and My Father are one."

—John 10:27–30 NKJV

LOVE CAME DOWN

Perhaps the most beautiful mystery of all is that of the Trinity—Father, Son, and Holy Spirit. Just when you think you might have a handle on it, you meditate on it again and it boggles your mind! All three Persons have always existed from eternity past, and they exist right here in the present and onward to the future and the Coming Age. Though the Father's presence was made manifest in numerous ways throughout the Old Testament, His presence in human form was limited to a few fleeting encounters.

His Spirit resided within the ark of the covenant and in the tabernacle first, and later within the temple in Jerusalem. But Israel did not stay faithful to the Lord—again and again they turned to worship other gods, other idols, forsaking their own God and His covenant with them. After repeated warnings of judgment for their prodigal ways, the Lord allowed their punishment to come through their exile to Babylon, after the complete destruction of the temple and of Jerusalem itself. Seventy years later, the exiles returned to Jerusalem and rebuilt the temple, but the Spirit of God did not return, and foreign powers continued to rule over the nation. For five hundred long years, Israel languished in utter darkness, with no God in the temple and no king of their own. For five hundred years, they were, quite literally, orphans. And *this* was the context into which Jesus, Immanuel, "God With Us," was born. Isaiah proclaims:

> Nevertheless, there will be no more gloom for those who were in distress. In the past he humbled the land of Zebulun and the land of Naphtali, but in the future he will honor Galilee of the nations, by the Way of the Sea, beyond the Jordan—

> The people walking in darkness have seen a great light; on those living in the land of deep darkness a light has dawned.
> You have enlarged the nation and increased their joy;
> they rejoice before you as people rejoice at the harvest, as warriors rejoice when dividing the plunder.

For as in the day of Midian's defeat, you have shattered
the yoke that burdens them,
the bar across their shoulders, the rod of their oppressor.
Every warrior's boot used in battle and every garment
rolled in blood
will be destined for burning, will be fuel for the fire.
For to us a child is born, to us a son is given, and the
government will be on his shoulders.
And he will be called Wonderful Counselor, Mighty
God, Everlasting Father, Prince of Peace.
Of the greatness of his government and peace there will
be no end.
He will reign on David's throne and over his kingdom,
establishing and upholding it with justice and
righteousness from that time on and forever.
The zeal of the LORD Almighty will accomplish this.

—Isaiah 9:1–7 NIV

The Father could not bear to watch His beloved suffer alone any longer. So the beautiful mystery of the Trinity began to unfold for all to see: The Father, King of the Universe, humbled Himself as the Son to be born helpless and vulnerable, just like us. He laid aside His divinity to become a man—a perfect example of a man—in order to teach us how to become sons, to show us the Father, and to lead the way back home to Him. And the *hesed* heart of the Father now beat inside Jesus, and for the first time the *hesed love* of the Father was demonstrated in the flesh. Glory to God!

JESUS IS A TRUE SON

Jesus is the way—*the only way*—to the Father. He teaches and demonstrates how our orphan hearts can be fully adopted as sons and daughters by showing us what a true son looks like. So if that is what we want, we must allow Jesus to lead the way. His whole life here on earth was spent teaching by example; He became one of us so that all of us could become like Him.

Though Jesus had taken on all the limitations of humanity, *He was completely secure in His identity* as the Son of God; He knew exactly who He was and where He stood with the Father at all times. For example, He did not argue with the devil in the wilderness when He was challenged, "*If* you *are* the Son of God …" He already knew He was! He simply redirected him back to the Father as the source of all provision, as the one who is sovereign and cannot be manipulated, and as the only one worthy of worship and service. The devil's tactic was to get Jesus to doubt His sonship first, so that He would succumb more easily to temptation. That is a powerful lesson for us! Jesus frequently affirms His identity as the Son of God, but He also does so modeling *complete submission to the Father's will*:

> "I tell you the truth, the Son can do nothing by himself. He does only what he sees the Father doing. Whatever the Father does, the Son also does. For the Father loves the Son and shows him everything he is doing. In fact, the Father will show him how to do even greater works than healing this man. Then you will truly be astonished."
>
> —John 5:19–20 NLT

"For I have come down from heaven to do the will of God who sent me, not to do my own will."

—John 6:38 NLT

"Do you not believe that I am in the Father, and the Father is in me? The words that I say to you, I do not speak on my own initiative, but the Father residing in me performs his miraculous deeds."

—John 14:10 NET

In fact, submission to the Father's will, in Jesus' own words, qualifies us as sons and daughters: "For *whoever does the will of my Father* in heaven *is my brother and sister and mother*" (Matthew 12:50).

A true son or daughter "looks like" his or her parents. Jesus said, "Whoever who has seen me has seen the Father" (John 14:9). Now, primarily Jesus meant that He and the Father are one and the same, but He is also saying that we can know what the Father is like by looking at the Son and what He does. As parents, most of us teach our children that they represent us (and the rest of the family) when they are somewhere off on their own. Hopefully my friends and acquaintances can say, "Yep, that's one of the Wuesthoff kids!" when they meet one of ours because they will espouse our family values, remember what they have been taught (and act accordingly), and even display some of the qualities that make our family unique and recognizable. It is the same with us as children of God. People ought to be able to recognize us as such, and Jesus shows us what those characteristics are. I've already mentioned a secure identity in Him and a complete submission to the Father's will, but these are other crucial attributes that identify us as true sons and daughters, as exemplified through the life of Jesus:

- **Love**: We must love the Father with all our heart, soul, mind, and strength, and we must love one another as we love ourselves, and as He has loved us (Mark 12:29–31). Jesus (and later, Paul) says that this commandment sums up the entire Law and everything the prophets advised and foretold—in other words, everything that was commanded in the Old Testament about love is contained and confirmed in this directive. If the Father is known by His love, so must His children be.

- **Forgiveness**: As children of God, we have done nothing to deserve forgiveness for our sins. Yet out of His great love, the Father forgives and keeps forgiving each time we ask and repent. So must we also forgive if we are to look like the Father.

- **Faith and Trust**: We must believe that our Father is a good father and we must believe <u>He is who He says He is</u>, and that <u>we are who He says we are</u>. We also must believe that <u>He can do everything He says He can do,</u> and that <u>we can do everything He says we can do</u>. That wording might be a little confusing—so reread it! It's important that we really get this. If we believe these things and act accordingly, we will look like Jesus and our Father.

- **Compassion**: Jesus (and therefore the Father) had compassion on the lost, the sick, the demon possessed, the outcast, the poor, the widows, and the orphans. We should, too.

These are, of course, only some of the characteristics of a true son or daughter, but they are definitely some of the most important. As I mentioned before, of our five children, four of them are adopted. It has always been fascinating to me to secretly study our biological son, noting the similarities and differences between him and us; how much he looks like me, how much he acts like my husband. He's inherited my husband's musical ability and my passion for God. But even more fascinating and wondrous have been our secret observations of our adopted children.

It is amazing to see, as they grow older, how many little quirks and traits, gifts and struggles, strengths and weaknesses they have also "inherited" from us over the years we have raised them. It's incredibly moving, actually, as well as a grave reminder of our responsibility to model that which we want them to inherit. The Father, as He showed Himself in the days of the Old Testament, was so magnificent, powerful, and "other worldly" that it was all but impossible to model Him or to live up to all He called His people to be. But then ... Jesus! Perfect though He was, Jesus humbled Himself completely to become one of us, so that through Him we could know how to look like Him, act like Him, and become like Him—true sons and daughters of the One Father.

JESUS MAKES US CLEAN

As I think about Jesus and what He must have been like when He lived among us over two thousand years ago, I marvel at the fact that, on the outside, Jesus looked like a regular guy. He had nothing distinctive about His appearance. His hair and clothing, accent, and mannerisms were probably indistinguishable from any other man His age in the Galilee. He was a tradesman, worked hard, spent lots of time outdoors. He probably got tanned and sweaty and dirty regularly—especially during the time of His ministry! But on the inside—in His heart, His mind, His will, and His emotions—Jesus was spotlessly clean. He was not only sinless but also whole and vibrant and overflowing with life, health, and soundness of mind and body.

These are the things He imparted to those He ministered to out of the power and overflow of what He carried on the inside. He continues to minister and impart those things now, to us and through us, as we are filled with His Spirit. And although He is completely willing to get His spotless hands dirty on our behalf—that is, to come to us while we are in our broken, sinful state—our dirt does not rub off on Him. That is why He can run to us and embrace us while we have been essentially living as slaves, mucking around with the pigs, filthy, starving, and a mess.

Then Jesus exchanges our dirty rags for a clean garment. He washes our feet and fits them with sandals. He stands before the Father alongside us and pronounces us clean and acceptable before Him. This is what His forgiveness and cleansing does for us. This is what His ultimate sacrifice and death on the cross has purchased for us. It not only affects the way we can see ourselves now that we are clean and the way we can live our lives in our new, forgiven state, it allows us to come before the Father *like Jesus*, a true son or daughter. Beloved, welcomed, accepted, and clean. And then we can come to the table together, and share in our Father's happiness.

"I Have Other Sheep That Are Not in This Sheepfold"

The above quote is one of my favorite sayings of Jesus. Why?

He's talking about you and me! And, in a sense, He is talking about adoption, which I have always been completely committed to and passionate about. Jesus often makes it clear during His ministry that He was sent only to "the lost sheep of Israel," the Jews. Still, He cannot resist the foreigners (Samarians, Romans) who come to Him in great faith. And in John 10, the teaching about the Good Shepherd, Jesus lets His followers know that the family of God is about to expand. This was not new teaching but a more pointed and current reminder of what the Old Testament prophets foretold:

> "I will also bless the foreigners who commit themselves
>   to the LORD,
> who serve him and love his name,
> who worship him and do not desecrate the Sabbath day
>   of rest,
> and who hold fast to my covenant.
> I will bring them to my holy mountain of Jerusalem
> and will fill them with joy in my house of prayer.
> I will accept their burnt offerings and sacrifices,
> because my Temple will be called a house of prayer for
>   all nations.
> For the Sovereign LORD,
> who brings back the outcasts of Israel, says:
> I will bring others, too,
> besides my people Israel."
>
> —Isaiah 56:6–8 NLT

We will talk more about the process of being brought "into the fold" in the next chapter, but right now I want to look at a few truths and myths about bringing the newly adopted into a family, and about adoption in general. I remember a few years back seeing a particular meme being circulated among animal lovers on Facebook. It was a photo of three identical-looking gray kittens all glancing toward a fourth kitten, black and white, with its face buried in its paws. The caption read, "He just found out he was adopted!" The kittens were cute, but the message it portrayed was not. I found myself shaking my head in disbelief that, even in our day and age, when all kinds of things in our culture have become commonplace and acceptable (some of them not good at all), being adopted still can be the punch line of a joke and still can have a stigma attached to it. Shame, embarrassment, being an outsider, being "less than." Nothing can be further from the truth.

All the way back in Exodus 2, when the infant Moses was adopted by Pharaoh's daughter, we can see the Lord using adoption as part of His plan for redemption. Though from the beginning it has been God's intention that all children would be welcomed, loved, and raised within their own biological families, and that all families who desire children would be able to conceive them, it has also been a reality almost from the very beginning that circumstances often prevent this from happening. Through adoption, He has provided a way to redeem what had been lost. David says the Lord is "father to the fatherless" and that "He sets the lonely into families," and we are commanded to take up the cause, defend, and provide for orphans—this is the kind of sacrifice the Lord desires and finds to be pleasing. We can see through the stories of Moses and Esther that God will use the placement of orphans in families, positionally, to accomplish His purposes.

What is precious to God cannot be used as a punch line or as an object of shame and embarrassment. And what about the adopted being outsiders or "less than"? Again, nothing can be further from the truth. When we adopted our last two children, they were ten and thirteen years old. Up until then, they had been bounced around most of their lives, living with various relatives and eventually in an orphanage. Our first three children at home (one biological, two adopted) have been with us from infancy. Neither of our first two daughters remembers life before us; we have been the only parents they have ever known. When our children from Uganda arrived, they arrived with the notion that there was a hierarchy within the family: our biological son being the most valuable and loved, the two girls who each arrived here as babies were next, and they were at the bottom—different than, other than, less than. You can imagine the issues that arose within our family right away—jealousy, competition, resentment, and much more. The first three kids had their issues, too; after all, the new kids got more attention and celebration, different rules (at first), and everything seemingly revolved and adjusted around them. The "new kids," of course, didn't see it that way at all!

It reminds me a little of the parable Jesus told His disciples of the workers in the vineyard. To paraphrase the story, a vineyard owner goes out early in the morning to hire day laborers and promises to pay them a denarius for their work. Every three hours, the master hires more workers until the last three hours of the day, promising each the same wage. When it comes time to receive their pay, the laborers who have been there the longest are offended that the other workers who have been there only a few hours are being paid the same day wage. It is the master's prerogative (since he's the one with the money) to decide how much to allot to each worker.

If we can substitute "father" for "boss" and "love/value" instead of "wages earned through service," you can see the analogy I'm drawing. I'm sure once the gospel message was available and accepted among the Gentiles, there was a bit of, "Hey, what gives? We were here first!" among the Jews that first followed Jesus. And there were probably a good number of Gentiles who thought they could not possibly be as loved and as valued by God as much as His chosen people (the Jews) were. But like the parable of the workers and like the parable of the prodigal son, how much God gives and whom He loves are not based on our merit, our bloodline, our position, or at what point we became part of the family. He simply loves us because He chooses to.

"I Choose You"

Being chosen is a very deep desire all of us have. It's a longing that cries out from our orphan hearts, and our experiences of being chosen—or not being chosen—constitute some of the most defining moments of our lives. We can all probably remember back to elementary school, lined up on the blacktop, waiting to be picked by either of the captains of the recess kickball teams. You may not remember anything else about those games, but I guarantee you remember what it felt like to be the last one standing after everyone else was chosen, if you were one of those unlucky kids.

How about being asked to the prom? Or running for school office, winning the MVP award, or getting a scholarship? Think about your engagement (if you're married) or your daydreams of what you might like that moment to feel like. There is something profoundly satisfying to our souls when we are chosen. The most meaningful and significant times, however, are not when we are chosen for something based on our own merit. We all like to be complimented on our achievements or on our special attributes, but there is always a deep knowing inside that those things are only temporary.

I'm grateful and happy, for instance, that my husband thinks I'm beautiful, but I am even more grateful that my appearance was not the sole basis for him choosing me as the one he wanted to marry. Your looks will inevitably change over time and something could happen to disrupt that, like an accident or illness. The same with talents, or even specific characteristics you may have.

Our newest children told us they could not figure out, when they were living at the orphanage, why they got the special attention I gave them when I came to visit, and why, out of the hundreds of children I knew in Uganda, they were the ones I wanted to adopt. It was hard to give to them a very specific answer. They weren't the "cutest" (though they certainly were cute!), the most talented, the friendliest, or from the most tragic background. I couldn't exactly say why, at first … I just *loved them.* As I've gotten to know them now that they are my children, I could tell you all sorts of things I love about them, why I think they are wonderful, why I would choose them all over again, knowing everything I know now. But the truth is, my husband and I just "chose to choose them," and we chose to love them, too. Loving them at times has been a conscious choice, rather than a feeling. It's very much the same as with all our other children and with each other, as a matter of fact.

The thing inherent about choice is that it is an act of will, a conscious exertion of power and influence over our thoughts that causes us to act upon it. And choosing to love is the most profound choice with the most far-reaching consequences we could ever make. Jesus did this for us. He chose to love us before the foundations of the world—before we were born, He chose us and He loved us. He was not satisfied with a few chosen sons and daughters … Adam, Eve, Noah, Abraham, Isaac, Jacob, Moses, Joshua, David. He was not satisfied with just a people, a tribe, or a nation. He began growing His family with Israel, yes, but His heart was for the nations, for *all* people.

He was not satisfied leaving us to our own devices, to our own best thinking, to our own inevitable destruction and eternal separation from Him—no! He was not satisfied until He came here in the flesh as one of us, to live with us in the flesh, to love on us in the flesh, to speak to us in our language, and to die as one of us *for all of us* in order to secure our place in His home forever. *Forever*, beloved, *He wants us with Him*. And He won't be satisfied until every tribe, people group, and individual has heard His message of hope and good news—the Good News that He loves us, that we belong, and that He wants us and chooses us to be His own children. This is love. This is His choice. *This is Jesus.*

Jesus, the Son of God, came to lead our way to the Father's heart and home forever. His life on earth showed us how to be a true son or daughter, how we could become clean and acceptable and holy before Him. He taught us that the Father's heart longed for all of us to be His children, and that we were loved and chosen by Him before we were even born. And as He went to the cross to purchase our salvation, redemption, and sonship, He made us this promise: *"I will not leave you as orphans; I will come to you."*

Come, Holy Spirit

The peace that passes all understanding is passing through me.
He appears without warning or announcement and blows through my weary soul.
Beautiful Ghost, would you settle and take your rest in me?
For it is rest that I need.
My weakened, worn-out, wrung-out heart has little to offer you now
except its pallid existence, but willing it is to receive you.
Be pleased, O Lord, to take all that I have—
my very spirit is a burnt offering to you.
Awaken the seeds of hope buried beneath this scorched earth;
Release new life that can only be set free through the test of fire.
Replace this eerie, wind-swept silence with stillness and peace—
more peace, I pray.
Comfort me, O Comforter, with the warmth of your presence;
may your breath displace the restless wanderings of my thoughts
with the assurance of security and calm.
Abide in me, be with me, take refuge to this refugee and be pleased to stay.

CHAPTER 4

Holy Spirit: Abba's Heart in Our Hearts

> For all who are led by the Spirit of God are children of God. For you did not receive a spirit of slavery to fall back into fear, but you have received a spirit of adoption. When we cry, "Abba! Father!" it is that very Spirit bearing witness with our spirit that we are children of God.
>
> —Romans 8:14–16 NRSV

Those verses above contain what I think is the best part of the Good News! The ongoing narrative of our story with God through the Scriptures is one that keeps getting better and better as it goes along, particularly from the cosmic turning point when the Lord Himself comes to us in the flesh through Jesus Christ the Son. This alone is more than anyone could have dreamed of—especially in the way it played out. While everyone (His disciples included) thought Jesus would become King of Israel and overthrow their Roman oppressors, leading Israel into the victorious outcome they were promised, God had a much bigger, better plan. Jesus would indeed reveal Himself to be King, but He would do so by overthrowing the kingdom of darkness and purchasing the salvation and freedom for all who would call upon His name as Lord and Savior. He defeated the power of sin and death through the cross and His resurrection from it, so that we could spend our eternity in the presence of God.

But again, He had an even bigger and better plan! He promised He would not leave us as orphans—He would come to us and send us "another Helper." The Paraclete, the Spirit of Truth, the Spirit of Adoption … the *Holy Spirit*. Poured out on display for all to see with the mind-blowing "baptism of fire" described in the book of Acts, we were given the Spirit of God Himself, not just to dwell *among* us, but to dwell *within* us. His radical choice of love to dwell inside us is a choice to continually testify—from His spirit to our spirit, from His heart to our heart—that we are His beloved children. When God sent His Holy Spirit to live inside us, He redeemed and restored back to us that intimate, spirit-to-spirit connection, that heart-to-heart communion that was lost back in the garden. This is the best news ever!

As with the Father and the Son, the Holy Spirit has existed within the Trinity from eternity past. The Spirit of the Lord is at work throughout the Old Testament, both as a demonstrated move of God that could be seen or felt, and as a physical presence that would come upon individuals (usually leaders like kings or prophets) to equip and empower them for certain tasks, giving them a supernatural anointing. In most ways, the work of the Holy Spirit has always been the same, whether in the Old or New

Testaments—He brings glory and honor to the Father and the Son, He gives revelation and speaks truth through prophecy and dreams, He anoints with power, gives wisdom and counsel, and is the creative force that gives birth to new things.

Amazingly, the death and resurrection of Jesus Christ not only gave us access to the Father, but it gave us permanent access to the Holy Spirit, too! When we come to Christ and believe in Him as Lord and Savior, we receive the Holy Spirit, the indwelling of God in our hearts. The Spirit Himself draws us to Jesus and gives us faith to believe, and when we do, He makes His home in us. That is the reality and permanent condition of the true believer in Christ. But wait … there's more! Once we have *received* the Holy Spirit, we can ask for more—to be *filled* with His Spirit. There is a big difference here. Just because we have something does not mean we are filled with it. Having money in your wallet isn't the same thing as your wallet being *filled* with money, right? Having love for someone isn't the same thing as being *filled* with love for that person. Having people at your party isn't the same thing as a house *full* of guests there to celebrate. Having good things is a blessing. But being *filled* with good things has the power to be life changing, the power to chart a new course, and the power that can enable us to step into something quite out of the ordinary. Impossibilities become possible; excitement replaces apathy.

One Spirit, Many Names

I love that our God is so indescribable that not even a host of names or adjectives can properly capture all He is. But I think especially with the Holy Spirit, who is, after all, *spirit,* it is helpful to get a handle on some of His names and functions, so we can know and understand Him better. Let's look at a few of them here, as they appear in Scripture.

The Spirit, As *Breath*

Here is the breath of God, the Spirit who gives and creates life:

> When no bush of the field was yet in the land and no small plant of the field had yet sprung up—for the LORD God had not caused it to rain on the land, and there was no man to work the ground, and a mist was going up from the land and was watering the whole face of the ground—then the LORD God formed the man of dust from the ground and *breathed into his nostrils the breath of life*, and the man became a living creature.
>
> —Genesis 2:5–7

> "But now, hear my speech, O Job,
> and listen to all my words.
> Behold, I open my mouth;
> the tongue in my mouth speaks.
> My words declare the uprightness of my heart,
> and what my lips know they speak sincerely.
> *The Spirit of God has made me,*
> *and the breath of the Almighty gives me life.*
>
> —Job 33:1–4

You send forth Your Spirit, they are created;
And You renew the face of the earth.
    —Psalm 104:30 NKJV

So Jesus said to them again, "Peace to you! As the Father has sent Me, I also send you." And when He had said this, *He breathed on them, and said to them, "Receive the Holy Spirit."*

    —John 20:21–22

The Spirit is the outbreathing of God, His inmost life going forth in a personal form to quicken. When we receive the Holy Spirit, we receive the inmost life of God Himself to dwell in a personal way in us. When we really grasp this thought, it is overwhelming in its solemnity. Just stop and think what it means to have the inmost life of that infinite and eternal Being whom we call God, dwelling in a personal way in you. How solemn and how awful and yet unspeakably glorious life becomes when we realize this.

    —R.A. Torrey[1]

Back in chapter 1, I wrote that the very breath of God gave Adam life and was in his lungs. We who have received the Holy Spirit share in that reality. Think of the very few instances that you actually share breath with another: rescue breathing, where you are attempting to restore life back to the person; and a kiss, one of the deepest, most passionate expressions of human intimacy. It is not too far a reach to say the Holy Spirit comes to us as a breath in very similar ways.

One of my favorite Bible stories is in Ezekiel 37. The Spirit of the Lord takes Ezekiel (in a vision) to a valley full of dry bones, the desiccated remains from a great battle. The Lord tells Ezekiel to prophesy to the bones and tell them to live—that the Sovereign Lord will breathe life into them. When he does this, the bones come together within bodies: muscle, tissue, and skin. They are animated and stand up and "come to life," but Ezekiel observes that there is no "breath" in them. So the Lord tells him, "'Prophesy to the breath; prophesy, son of man, and say to the breath, Thus says the Lord GOD: Come from the four winds, O breath, and breathe on these slain, that they may live'" (Ezekiel 37:9). In this vision, the Lord is not only giving Ezekiel encouragement that, by the Spirit of the Lord, the Jews exiled in Babylon would indeed come together and live again in their own land, but He is also foretelling the coming resurrection of the faithful. When the Lord tells Ezekiel to "prophesy to the breath" he is telling him to prophesy to the *Spirit*, to encourage and stir up the Spirit with what the Father is about to do through Him! Even more mind-boggling is the Lord calling Ezekiel "son of man" (which is the title Jesus gives Himself), so the whole passage is a greater prophecy that soon the Father, *through* the Son, *by* the Holy Spirit, will breathe new life into all who come to Him and give us new, eternal life through His resurrection!

THE SPIRIT OF TRUTH

"I will ask the Father, and He will give you another Helper, that He may be with you forever; that is *the Spirit of truth*, whom the world cannot receive, because it does not see Him or know Him, but you know Him because He abides with you and will be in you."

—John 14:16–17 NASB

"When the Helper comes, whom I will send to you from the Father, that is the *Spirit of truth who proceeds from the Father*, He will testify about Me, and you will testify also, because you have been with Me from the beginning."

—John 15:26–27 NASB

"I still have many things to say to you, but you cannot bear them now. When the *Spirit of truth* comes, he will guide you into all the truth, for he will not speak on his own authority, but whatever he hears he will speak, and he will declare to you the things that are to come. He will glorify me, for he will take what is mine and declare it to you. All that the Father has is mine; therefore I said that he will take what is mine and declare it to you."

—John 16:12–16

We are from God. Whoever knows God listens to us; whoever is not from God does not listen to us. By this we know the *Spirit of truth* and the spirit of error.

—1 John 4:6

The Bible assures us that it is impossible for God to lie (Numbers 23:19; 1 Samuel 15:29; Hebrews 6:18), so it makes perfect sense that His Spirit is called the Spirit of Truth. When we receive the Holy Spirit and walk in the fullness of His revelation, we have assurance that God will help us to discern what is true and to be able to live according to His truth. This is crucial in being able to defeat the many lies we believe and have come into agreement with, whispered to us by Satan, the deceiver, the author of lies. Neil Anderson, author of *Victory Over the Darkness* and many other books on spiritual freedom, says,

> If I were to tempt you, you would know it. If I were to accuse you, you would know it. But if I were to deceive you, you wouldn't know it. The power of Satan is in the lie. If you remove the lie you remove the power.[2]

We cannot recognize, never mind remove, the lies we believe without the help of the Spirit of Truth. This is especially important when it comes to leading our orphan hearts to the Father, because much of what we believe about ourselves, our lives, and about God are simply untrue. If we lived our lives with the secure knowledge that we not only have access to the Spirit of Truth but also that He actually *lives inside us*, it would radically change our lives! It would be impossible for it *not* to! Jesus made an incredible promise to us: He said He would send us another Helper called the Spirit of Truth. The Holy Spirit, as Helper, helps us to *receive* Him as Spirit of Truth, and to *believe* Him as Spirit of Truth. We are not left to our own power and ability to discern and believe and live out the Truth of God—the Holy Spirit helps us to do just that. The second part of what Jesus promises us is equally incredible: that the Spirit of Truth will stay with us *forever*. We may become confused or deceived or lose our handle on the Truth, but we do not lose the Spirit of Truth within us. We just have to remember and believe that we already have access to Him and all that comes with His permanent presence within us.

THE PARACLETE: OUR HELPER, ADVOCATE, COUNSELOR, INTERCESSOR, AND COMFORTER

> If you love me, keep my commandments. And I will ask the Father, and he shall give you another *Paraclete*, that he may abide with you for ever.
>
> —John 14:15–16 DRA

> But the *Paraclete*, the Holy Ghost, whom the Father will send in my name, he will teach you all things, and bring all things to your mind, whatsoever I shall have said to you.
>
> —John 14:26 DRA

> But I tell you the truth: it is expedient to you that I go: for if I go not, the *Paraclete* will not come to you; but if I go, I will send him to you.
>
> —John 16:7 DRA

Another name given to the Holy Spirit is "the Paraclete," which comes from the Greek word *parakletos*, meaning "called to one's side." Different biblical translations use a variety of English nouns (like those listed in the main heading) to describe the Holy Spirit's function, depending on the context of what is being said. I often think of the Paraclete as the "whisper of God" within my spirit, the voice that guides and directs me, especially in times when I feel confused, burdened, or unsettled. He also guides and directs my prayers, both prayers that I pray myself, and those that I pray over others. Revelation of His wisdom, words of knowledge, and prophetic words come from the Paraclete.

One of the most beautiful attributes of the Lord is His desire to draw close to us. From breaking through with powerful manifestations and encounters with His presence in Old Testament times, to physically intersecting our world and walking alongside us through Jesus, the Lord desired to draw even closer ... to actually become *part* of us, and for us to become part of Him! As I mentioned before, the Spirit of God used to dwell within the tabernacle and later the temple, specifically within the innermost chamber known as the "holy of holies." Once a year, the high priest would prepare himself to go behind the curtain into the chamber, to offer worship through sacrifice on behalf of the people. It was customary for attendants to tie a rope to the ankle of the high priest, so if the priest died in the Presence, they could pull him out without risking death themselves. The Holy Spirit really is that holy. But with the death of Jesus and His sacrifice becoming the atonement for our sins once and for all, the curtain of the temple was torn in two—creating permanent access to the Spirit of the Lord, forever! Now the Spirit of God dwells within us—*we are the temple and the innermost chamber is in our own hearts!* Author and theologian N. T. Wright says, "Those in whom the Spirit comes to live are God's new Temple. They are, individually and corporately, places where heaven and earth meet."[3] Heaven and earth *meet within us* ... the kingdom of God *resides within us*! This is truth that has the power to overthrow the lies that bind the orphan heart!

THE SPIRIT OF ADOPTION

For all who are led by the Spirit of God are sons of God. For you did not receive the spirit of slavery to fall back into fear, but you have received the *Spirit of adoption* as sons, by whom we cry, "Abba! Father!" The Spirit himself bears witness with our spirit that we are children of God, and if children, then heirs—heirs of God and fellow heirs with Christ, provided we suffer with him in order that we may also be glorified with him.

—Romans 8:14–17

They are Israelites, and *to them belong the adoption*, the glory, the covenants, the giving of the law, the worship, and the promises. To them belong the patriarchs, and from their race, according to the flesh, is the Christ, who is God over all, blessed forever. Amen. But it is not as though the word of God has failed. For not all who are descended from Israel belong to Israel, and not all are children of Abraham because they are his offspring, but "Through Isaac shall your offspring be named." This means that *it is not the children of the flesh who are the children of God, but the children of the promise are counted as offspring.*

—Romans 9:4–8

But when the fullness of time had come, God sent forth his Son, born of woman, born under the law, to redeem those who were under the law, so that *we might receive adoption as sons. And because you are sons, God has sent the Spirit of his Son into our hearts, crying, "Abba! Father!"* So you are no longer a slave, but a son, and if a son, then an heir through God.

—Galatians 4:4–7

In love *he predestined us for adoption to himself as sons* through Jesus Christ, according to the purpose of his will, to the praise of his glorious grace, with which he has blessed us in the Beloved.

—Ephesians 1:4–6

The Spirit of Adoption is perhaps my favorite attribute and name of the Holy Spirit. Among other things, He reminds us who we are and where we stand with the Father. I love how Scripture says that we have "received" adoption. That's because our adoption as sons and daughters isn't something we can earn or demand. It is a gift of love—an invitation into deep relationship and belonging, and into receiving an unimaginably good inheritance. The Spirit of Adoption is an identity maker and an identity sustainer. He is the opposite of (and the antidote to) the spirit of fear and the spirit of slavery. But above all, the Spirit of Adoption brings the heart of the Father to our hearts, and in that He gives us a heart-to-heart revelation of His love (think *hesed!*).

Paul says in Romans and in Galatians that it is by His Spirit that we can cry, "*Abba!* Father!" There has been some debate about the meaning of *Abba* in these verses—I have read some controversy about the teaching that *Abba* means "Daddy" or "Papa" or other childlike terms of endearment for a father. In truth, it is used like

that now, in modern Hebrew, though in its original Aramaic in Jesus' time it did not carry that specific (diminutive) meaning. The point is, however, that in Aramaic, *Abba* was the specific name to address *one's own father* directly, rather than the broader label, "Father" (*Pater* in the Greek), used more generically as a term of respect for anyone who was a father or in an authority position.[4] So Paul is saying that it is because of the Spirit of Adoption that we can call God *"Abba"* as *true sons and daughters*, not just "Father" out of respect for His authority and lordship. The Spirit Himself testifies this to us and cries it out for us, even when we cannot yet recognize our place with Him. And that is part of the heart-to-heart revelation of His love—even when we can't see it, the *hesed* heart of God now resides within us, reminding us we are His children. But when we are able to recognize it and join with the Holy Spirit, we truly *can* cry out, "*Abba!* Daddy! Papa!" or any other affectionate name we would like to call our real father. For indeed, He is as real as real gets.

"THE CURE"

As I reflect on the person and work of the Holy Spirit, I've noticed I have now begun to think of Him as "the cure." Maybe it's more of a realization that it's actually true. What good parent doesn't want to fix anything he or she can that is hurting their child? When they get a scraped knee or their first beesting, we scoop them up and console them, but we also look to clean the wound and bind it so it will heal. When our children experience a crushing loss or bitter disappointment, our hearts just break for them, don't they? Again, we comfort and try to counsel and encourage, but if we could really fix it for them, wouldn't we?

The Lord is like that, too, except infinitely more loving and wise and capable of real help. He *is* the help and His Spirit is right there ready to administer it. He's the cure for our chronic sickness from sin; He's the cure for our weaknesses and our failings. Whatever we lack, He supplies. When we can't even pray, He prays for us on our behalf. He teaches what we do not know, points the way when we are lost. He corrects us when we are wrong, and gives us what we need, often before we even know we need it. When we are desperate, He is comfort and hope. The Holy Spirit, the Helper, the Comforter, the Intercessor, the Paraclete, the Spirit of Truth, the Spirit of Wisdom, the Spirit of Adoption … whatever our ailment, He is the cure. And very specific to the topic at hand, *He is the cure for the orphan heart.* Remember the four chambers?

- For our soul loneliness, He is the cure.

- He comes alongside us, dwells within us, and never leaves. He brings the fellowship of the Trinity into our very hearts, so that Jesus and the Father are there as well.

- For our restless wandering, He is the cure.

- He brings us peace and rest, for He is the embodiment of those things. With wisdom and discernment, He points the way we should go—the way to the Father, the way home.

- He is the cure for our shame.

- He dispels the lies that fuel our shame, because He is the Spirit of Truth. He covers our nakedness with righteousness, as He shows us Jesus in the mirror of our hearts. He testifies to us that we are sons and daughters of a loving Father, and in Him there is no shame.

- He is the cure for the spirit of fear.

- As the Spirit of Adoption, He drives out fear with His love and leaves security and safety in its place. He teaches us that our true home is with the Father and we are His beloved children. We belong to Him and we are safe.

The Holy Spirit helps us know the Father and to follow Jesus. He teaches us how to be His disciples and how to show the Father's heart to the rest of the world. He is our Helper in every sense of the word, so close within us He is only a breath or a heartbeat away. While He is an ever-present presence within us, He is pleased to pour in more of Himself if we ask. And when we ask, He comes to us—sometimes in a blanket of peace and comfort, sometimes in waves of unspeakable love, sometimes with power to overwhelm the darkness in and around us with purifying, cleansing light. And we can be filled over and over again, born anew each day with a fresh supply of healing power, so that not only can we experience the cure, we can administer it to others around us with the overflow of His goodness.

Grafted In

Take me in into Your presence,
surround me with Your love;
tell me I belong to You,
set my mind on things above.

O Father to the fatherless,
adopt me as Your own!
Blessed Trinity, be my family,
let Your love become my home.

Nowhere on earth can be found
what only You provide;
You satisfy my every need—
in You I trust, I hide.

Change my thoughts, my life, my identity
to that which You declare:
"Child of God, grafted in forever"
Forever, Lord, keep me there!

CHAPTER 5

Get Ready to Get Radical

And you Gentiles, who were branches from a wild olive tree, have been grafted in. So now you also receive the blessing God has promised Abraham and his children, sharing in the rich nourishment from the root of God's special olive tree. But you must not brag about being grafted in to replace the branches that were broken off. You are just a branch, not the root.

"Well," you may say, "those branches were broken off to make room for me." Yes, but remember—those branches were broken off because they didn't believe in Christ, and you are there because you do believe. So don't think highly of yourself, but fear what could happen. For if God did not spare the original branches, he won't spare you either.

Notice how God is both kind and severe. He is severe toward those who disobeyed, but kind to you if you continue to trust in his kindness. But if you stop trusting, you also will be cut off. And if the people of Israel turn from their unbelief, they will be grafted in again, for God has the power to graft them back into the tree. You, by nature, were a branch cut from a wild olive tree. So if God was willing to do something contrary to nature by grafting you into his cultivated tree, he will be far more eager to graft the original branches back into the tree where they belong.

—Romans 11:17–24 NLT

This is a fairly lengthy passage to begin this chapter with, and you may be wondering why it is appearing here in a chapter on getting radical. I'm including it because it is one of the most beautiful illustrations of adoption that I know. In fact, the grafted-branch-into-the-family-tree analogy is commonly used in adoption circles; how much more meaningful and sobering it is to read about it in God's Word! So, let's unpack this a bit, starting with the analogy itself.

THE GRAFTING PROCESS

What is grafting? Grafting is a common horticultural practice to combine two or more plants (usually fruit trees) in order to improve the health, appearance, or functionality of the plant. It was very common, especially in biblical times, to graft olive trees in order to produce better fruit. Wild olive trees were hardy, robust, and had very sturdy root systems, but the olives they produced were small with large pits and bitter flesh. Olive trees that had been cultivated over time produced large fruit, good for eating and making oil, which of course was valuable for its many uses. So olive growers would cut branches from cultivated trees and graft them into the trunks (and root systems) of wild trees. The grafting process went like this:

The wild olive tree would be cut, more than halfway down from top to bottom, as far down as would remain only a "Y" shape—the trunk and two main branches. What was once a beautiful, vibrant tree was reduced to a seemingly lifeless, ugly stump—a truly brutal process for the host tree. Then the grower would come with branches from the cultivated olive tree, cut small slots into the two main branches, and place the new branches inside, bind them up to protect them, and let nature take its course. Soon, the cultivated branches would send roots down to join with the host tree, and over time, the two segments "merge" and grow together into one tree. The grafted branches become part of the main trunk and are fed by the host tree's root system, but interestingly, they always continue to retain their original properties: rather than becoming a hybrid, the grafting process actually changes the whole identity of the tree.[1]

In Romans 11, Paul is writing to an audience who is familiar with this process, but notice that he has flipped around the analogy so that the wild olive branches are grafted into the cultivated tree. This would have been counterintuitive (radical!) and not at all what people would expect. I'm sure this got their attention, and Paul was illustrating for them that the cultivated tree represents God's covenant people (the Lord Himself is the root system) and the natural branches that grow from the tree are the Jews. But we (Gentiles) are the wild olive branches, cut from our wild, independent, self-sufficient, seemingly sturdy roots, and through Christ we have been grafted into the cultivated, covenantal family tree of God. Our roots will grow down into the trunk until we begin to be fed by the roots of our Host. Then we become one with the tree, bearing our own unique properties and fruit, but now our identity becomes that of the cultivated tree, which is the family of God. Paul's warning to the Gentiles is not to assume the branches of the Jews were only pruned to make room for them, and not to be tempted to boast of their newfound position on the tree, because unless their roots grow deep into the tree themselves, their branches will die or be cut off. He also reminds them that any branches that have been cut can be grafted back in at any time by the Lord.

THE FAMILY TREE

The Wuesthoff family tree has taken on a very unique identity. Most of my husband's family has been in America for many generations, some since the Mayflower pilgrims arrived on Massachusetts soil. My ancestors came to this country more recently; my grandparents and great-grandparents immigrated within the last century or so. So our biological son became a mix of Italian, English, Irish, German, and Hungarian stock—a true hybrid species himself! And then we grafted into our family tree two Korean branches and two Ugandan branches.

As adoptive parents, we believe and teach that our children retain all that they were born to be: their races, their ethnicities, their unique biological makeup and personality traits they inherited from their natural parents. They have gifts and abilities that stem from their own ancestral lines; their destinies and purposes very well may arise out of their own family histories. Like the wild olive branches, the fruit they bear will have their own unique properties and flavors. But since they are now grafted into the Wuesthoff tree, they also inherit the blessings, destinies, and purposes God has intended through that family line. Our children are fed by us not only in the physical sense but also emotionally, spiritually, and relationally. Their branches, though their own, will take on characteristics and properties of their new host tree, and with God's help their identities will become firmly rooted in being our children, in being a true part of our family.

This is a two-way process: the host tree must accept the branches as part of its own, and the branches must send down roots into the tree. As with real grafting, this process has to be carefully nurtured and protected until it's complete. I've read and heard from other parents who have adopted older children that "three years home" is sort of a benchmark when your family starts to feel like a real family unit. I remember praying for that time to come quickly early on when things were really difficult. Now that our children have been home a little over five years, I can testify that the timing seems about right. We feel gelled, complete, "normal"—at least as normal as a family like ours gets! Incredibly, as I researched the grafting process for olive trees, I learned that the new branches also become fully grafted in and begin to produce their fruit about three years later. God is truly amazing. I love how He buries some of His truths for us to discover!

GETTING READY TO GET RADICAL

Now back to you. Though we have all been born with orphan hearts, we have not all traveled the same roads on our journey; some of us will find it easier than others to embrace our adoption by the Father and find our home in Him. I wish a smooth and painless journey for all who seek it, and maybe some of you will find it to be so. But if you are anything like me, the process to understand and embrace God as Father and to see ourselves as a true son or daughter may be frustrating, difficult, and at times painful. There were times I had little hope I would ever feel God's complete love and acceptance or that He would ever fully inhabit the gaping hole that ached to be filled. If that sounds like you, take heart. There is hope, I promise. What's more, the Father promises it, and He never lies or breaks His promise. He never has; He never will. Hebrews 6:19 tells us we can anchor ourselves in that hope.

However, if you truly want to live a radically transformed life, you will probably have to prepare yourself to get a little radical. If you want change, you have to make changes. That sounds like a no-brainer, but when it comes down to it, most of us hate change. It's uncomfortable and often messy. Sometimes it takes a whole lot longer with a lot more effort involved than you hoped it would. But as one of my favorite song lyrics (by Bruce Cockburn) says, "Nothing worth having comes without a fight//Gotta kick at the darkness 'til it bleeds daylight."[2]

In the following chapters, I will outline and expand upon some steps to lead your orphan heart home to the Father's heart, where you can know that you know that you *know* you have been grafted in. Hopefully, some of those steps will take you great distances toward your destination. I will share insights I have gained through my experience as an adoptive parent seeking to understand my own adoption, and some words and ways God has spoken to me in order to teach me how to get there. Some of my specific steps may work perfectly for you and some you may have to adapt to fit your unique story and personality. But don't dismiss anything because it seems trivial, silly, or uncomfortable—remember, you may just have to get radical. I did. And it has been so worth every ounce of effort, and the Lord has been gracious, loving, and kind beyond anything I have experienced before.

Our loving Father never intended for us to be orphans, but we have inherited that condition from our first parents, and on some level we continue to choose our orphan-ness again and again, because we have not learned another way. Our hearts function from a place of soul loneliness, restless wandering, shame, and fear. We try to fill our empty places by hustling for what we need, surrendering to hopelessness and despair, trying to be good enough, or allowing ourselves to become jaded and disillusioned by disappointment in order to protect ourselves from more hurt. But those things just don't work. We were created—hardwired— for sonship and belonging, and we will never stop longing for it (or running from it) until we realize that *we have been grafted in*. We are lavishly loved by a Father with a *hesed* heart, pursued and chosen by a Savior, Jesus, who died on our behalf so we could run into our Father's arms, clean and accepted. Best of all, we have received the very heart of our Abba Father within our own hearts by the Spirit of Adoption, who helps us in every way we need. The Lord has seen to it that we have everything we need to equip us for our journey home, where we belong.

Song of the Overcomer

I am worth something.
I am a fighter and a pursuer and a lover
and I don't give up.
So many times I have fallen on my own accord,
many other times have I been knocked down—
abused,
betrayed,
rejected,
abandoned—
but still, I press on.
Though well-acquainted with loss, I possess much which cannot be stolen;
I bear the handprint of my Creator on my heart.
I am that smoldering wick that will not be snuffed out.
I know what I am longing for, living for, striving for.
These now are the things that define me:
hope,
beauty,
love,
resurrection.
So I run, headlong, towards my Savior's open arms and I fall down at his feet.
In abject humility I worship him, but I cannot resist lifting my face towards his.
I want to stare deep in his eyes and let his liquid love pour into my whole being,
filling every empty place to overflowing, never stopping.
And I notice that I can see my own reflection in those eyes.
She is happy and whole and smiling back at me.
She is freedom.
She is joy.
And she is very much alive.

CHAPTER 6

My Adoption Story

While he was still speaking, there came from the ruler's house some who said, "Your daughter is dead. Why trouble the Teacher any further?" But overhearing what they said, Jesus said to the ruler of the synagogue, "Do not fear, only believe." And he allowed no one to follow him except Peter and James and John the brother of James. They came to the house of the ruler of the synagogue, and Jesus saw a commotion, people weeping and wailing loudly. And when he had entered, he said to them, "Why are you making a commotion and weeping? The child is not dead but sleeping." And they laughed at him. But he put them all outside and took the child's father and mother and those who were with him and went in where the child was. Taking her by the hand he said to her, "Talitha cumi," which means, "Little girl, I say to you, arise." And immediately the girl got up and began walking (for she was twelve years of age), and they were immediately overcome with amazement.

—Mark 5:35–42

I Died A Thousand Deaths

I began this book at the lowest point of my journey, a colossal mental breakdown on my front lawn. But as I said, that was a turning point, not a starting point. Much had come before it that led me to such a desperate place. I had suffered deeply that year, probably more than at any other point in my life. My heart had been broken in more ways than I ever thought possible, and I felt as though I had already died a thousand deaths. A good number of those deaths involved losses so great I felt like pieces of me were being carried away with each loss. Then there were deaths of hopes, the deaths of dreams, plans, aspirations ... even memories. All the while I had continued to function, walking around wounded and vulnerable, largely unprotected from the usual hurts and disappointments that come our way. And as those little zingers found their way deep in the throbbing, raw places, I'd die all over again. Daily life had become a steep, uphill climb—often like scaling a foreboding cliff wall—and with each loss, I had fewer and fewer handholds to cling to. In complete despair and hopelessness, I finally let go. Ironically, it was letting go of the things I had been clinging to that ultimately saved me.

Let me explain.

Throughout my entire life, and even though I was not aware of it, I can confidently say that I have lived with an orphan heart. Inside, I was desperate to belong to something or someone who would make me feel loved, valuable, worthy, and secure. Though my orphan heart was an inherited condition to begin with, many of my life's experiences served to reinforce its themes, traits, and strongholds, so that it became a deeply entrenched identity for me. I had always been committed to people and relationships but usually felt rejected and abandoned by them. I received much prayer, ministry, and counseling over the years to address the different issues that would crop up and interfere with my life, but their root cause (an orphan heart) was never identified. Even in all my reading and exposure to excellent biblical teaching, I had never even heard the term before.

Three things brought this root condition to the forefront, beginning in 2013.

The first was the terminal sickness and impending death of my best friend. I have been blessed with many precious friends, but this one held a unique place in my life. Through her steadfast love and dedicated friendship, she helped me begin to understand who I was and why I was valuable. She had a way of being able to accurately put her finger on my gifts and my struggles, help me bring them to the forefront, and then bring them before Jesus. Through her friendship, I grew immensely in many areas of my life. We had a David-and-Jonathan, covenantal kind of relationship; she was a friend who was closer than a sister. And as she was dying, I knew my very foundation was being shaken. I was consumed by grief and fear and terrified of losing her, partly because I felt like I was losing myself in the process. One afternoon, I lay facedown in the sanctuary of my church, pleading for the Lord to save her life, when He spoke to me: *My child, you have an orphan spirit.* I did not understand what that meant or why He said it, but I filed it away in my memory, to investigate it later.

"You Are Very Much Like Her"

The second circumstance that highlighted my orphan heart was also happening during the same time period that my friend was dying. We had just adopted two older children, expanding our family from three to five kids—we now had one biological and four adopted children. We adopted our first two daughters (separately) as infants from Korea, and our new son and daughter were biological siblings from Uganda. Including our biological son, we now had three girls and two boys, children of three races from three different continents. To say this was a challenging time is an understatement! Our two new children, who were ten and thirteen at the time, had a traumatic history before they came home with us. Naturally, there were a whole host of things to learn about, adjust to, and work through as they became acclimated to a radically new and different life within our family.

As much as we tried to prepare and educate ourselves to be good, effective, and loving parents to them, my husband and I quickly realized just how ill-equipped we were. In His grace and mercy, the Lord told me clearly that He would teach and lead us through the process of parenting them, so I was to turn all my questions over to Him, listen up, and learn. Big lessons lay ahead. Somewhere early in this process, I understood two things well: one, that our main job (aside from loving them and meeting their needs) was to teach them what it really means to be adopted; and two, that I had no real understanding or any experience to draw from personally. I did not know what "being adopted" meant for myself. One day, while crying out to the Lord in frustration about our newest daughter's behavior, He replied to me, *"You know, you are very much like her."* I was shocked. I couldn't see the parallels at all. But God had spoken so clearly, I began to ask Him to show me how. And little by little, He did. But as we continued to walk out our difficult parenting journey, our lives took an ugly turn.

This third circumstance ripped me apart and exposed my

orphan heart clearly for all to see. Within a year of my friend's death, I lost our beloved church and most of the relationships my husband and I had built there over the twenty-plus years we attended. I became the focus of a church scandal—an almost literal scapegoat for the sins of the leadership. In Old Testament times, the Levitical high priest would symbolically place the sins of the community onto a goat, and then cast it off into the wilderness. Without explanation or any direct communication, the church pushed me and my family out and permanently shut the door behind us. It was only months later that I began to understand what they had done and heard the twisted narrative that had been circulated about me. I not only lost a staggering number of relationships but also my ministry, my church home, and my reputation. I was so grief-stricken I could hardly breathe, and when we finally lost the friendship of the couple who had walked with us through the worst of it, I could take no more, and I collapsed into the bushes outside our home.

THE JOURNEY TO LEAD MY OWN HEART HOME

If we have eyes to see it, I think God often uses these times of intense suffering to invite us to put to death the things in our lives that contribute to, or are even the by-products of, the pain we are currently experiencing. Though I did not see it at the time, my meltdown on the lawn was the first step in letting go of the things I was holding on to. Not that I chose it, really—I was losing them against my will—but I came to the point where I had no strength left to even try to hold on to them. And as I fell from that precarious cliff, the Father caught me and saved me like only He can. I was already dead (like Jairus's daughter in the Scripture above), and the

Lord cleared the room of all those who would doubt or interfere with my resurrection, and He said to me, *"Talitha, cumi. Little girl, I say to you, arise."*

And so, here we are back again at the turning point, the beginning of my journey to embrace my "sonship." He has been so good to teach me, step by step, how to lead my orphan heart home to Him, the Spirit of Adoption. He's given me unique insights into how to navigate the brokenness, identify the patterns, and teach new ways of thinking and behaving. Though at times I can still be encumbered by my own brokenness, I am now healing and growing into a new understanding—and better still, a new reality—of living life as a fully-adopted child of God. I know now that I have been *grafted in*. I am rising up, overcoming. I pray that my journey will bless and equip you for yours.

Letting Go

I'm letting go of the dream, the hope, the desires of the old me—
the me that was formed and raised in the clutches of uncertainty
and in the seductive lure of hopelessness.
Those dreams, albeit core and foundational longings of the heart,
are ones made too small and narrow by former realities,
the shadows or refracted images of what is now possible and true.
So I must let go of the old dream to make room for the new:
the new possibilities,
the new dreams,
a new hope.
For hope is arising within me; it springs forth, promising a full bloom.
Why should I let my thoughts linger on former days spent hiding from the storm,
watching the rain from the window and praying for the clouds to part
and make way for the sun?
No, the Truth now lies in springtime warmth,
the beauty and hope that is right here before me.
The Lord has drawn my dreams of old like a needle and thread
through the curtain that marks entry into a greater Kingdom reality.
So, while the essence of the dream remains,
it changes shape and form to reflect a new paradigm,
and the promise of what has been hoped for now awaits me there.
It is real and tangible and true, but my eyes and heart must recognize it
in order to lay hold of it with both hands.

I cannot be torn between two worlds: one that is constrained by the limits of brokenness, and one that offers life and fullness and endless possibilities, made possible by the One who has made me.
I stand over the gap of a deep and frightening chasm,
one hand clasping, grasping
at the now-present-future Truth that offers itself to me.
My grip on the side behind me is weak and tenuous;
still I must risk letting go of what's behind
to take hold of the Truth with both hands.
So this I choose; this I must do:
(deep breath) *I am letting go.*

CHAPTER 7

The Four S's: Strongholds, Sacrifice, Sanctification, and Surrender

My soul is like a house, small for you to enter, but I pray you to enlarge it. It is in ruins, but I ask you to remake it. It contains much that you will not be pleased to see: this I know and do not hide. But who is to rid it of these things? There is no one but you.

—Augustine di Hippo, *Confessions*[1]

I have never been one to ease into things. Once I have an awareness of what the ultimate goal is, I usually look for the most direct way to get there. That's rarely the easy way! But in matters such as emotional or spiritual healing and growth, time and time again I have found this to be the best way. One of my own personal mantras—one I truly believe in and remind myself of often—is *once you know something, you become responsible for it.* Let me explain that a little. We make a whole lot of mistakes and step into a whole lot of sinful patterns and behaviors because we are ignorant of some aspect of truth; we do them unknowingly. There is a certain amount of grace for that, but sooner or later someone or something will call your attention to your error and you become fully aware of it. Consequently, you become responsible for what you now know. If you repeat the same mistakes or sins, it points to a bigger problem, like patterns of avoidance, denial, addiction, and so on. In my experience, once you become aware that something isn't right, that is the time to go after identifying and solving the problem, before it becomes something so big it drags you or someone else down into it deeper. Does that mean I am always able to take care of my own messes before they get out of hand? Obviously not, if I have to repeat that mantra to myself! But it is a motivator, and when that "someone or something" that calls your attention to a matter is the Holy Spirit, it's best to attend to it ASAP.

So that's where I was a few years ago. I was aware of and had been dealing with various issues for a while, but I hadn't really been able to get at the root of it all. When the Lord whispered, *"You have an orphan spirit"* to me, it was because He knew I was headed for a major fall, and I would need to know what the root cause was when it happened. Well, it did happen, and it was major. Within a year or so following that word from God, I lost my best friend to cancer, had a health condition of my own that touched off months of panic attacks, and then experienced that series of devastating losses—all of which led to a complete emotional collapse. Everything on the inside fell apart, and life on the outside was barely holding together. I could not find my footing at all because my foundation was being shaken, and my foundation was more like a house of cards than one made of bricks and mortar. That was not to say I didn't know or love the Lord—I did, and I had a deep faith. But my faith, knowledge, and love for the Lord was not secured in my identity as a child of the Father; my identity was that of an orphan. The orphan identity of fear, shame, soul loneliness, and restless wandering *was* my foundation, and it was ultimately what rose up and took over when the biggest fear I had—staggering, overwhelming loss—triggered my downfall.

EXCAVATION IS NECESSARY

For a number of years, the house across the street from us was a boarded-up eyesore, uninhabitable and condemned. Its owner had passed away, and when she did, her drug-dealing son and his buddies turned the otherwise decent-looking Cape Cod into a crack house. No maintenance was done to the house and yard after that, and when the drug money wasn't coming in, the young men began dismantling anything in the house that could be sold for a quick buck: first the copper plumbing, then the kitchen cabinets, and eventually they got really desperate and sold the gutters and pool fencing for their aluminum. The house was a ramshackle mess, and eventually the city kicked the men out and condemned the building. And then it stood there for two years, an ugly blight in our nice little neighborhood. One day, they finally came to knock it down, and my kids and I sat in front of the picture window, watching them like TV. It was pretty amazing to witness. I had seen buildings demolished before, but never ones that were still full of the stuff houses become filled with over the years. We watched with fascination as the excavator pulled out broken boards, bedsheets, mattresses, clothes—all kinds of junk that had been left behind. When all the rubble was cleared, they just backfilled the foundation and buried it. I thought, *How will they ever be able to build a new house with that there?* Well, the answer is they couldn't. Months later, the land was sold at auction to a builder, and before any construction could be done, they had to dig up that old foundation and tear it out; then they could replace it with a new, sturdy one, upon which a new house could be built.

This is how I needed to begin my process; perhaps this is where you are also. I needed to tear out and replace my old foundation with a new one, but there was a lot of junk in the way that needed to be excavated before we could get all the way down there. I say "we" because I was not capable of doing it myself. I had a Helper. As Augustine confessed to the Lord, "But who is to get rid of these things? There is no one but you." Hopefully, if you've reached this point in the book, you are ready to begin your process, too. So, with the Holy Spirit as our Helper and Jesus as our guide and example, let's begin to look at the steps along the journey.

#1: Tearing Down Strongholds

Depending on how well you have "maintained your house" (to use the above illustration), there may be a little or a lot of stuff to sift through and get rid of. Some things are relatively easy to take care of; some are bigger and more powerful. These are referred to as *strongholds*. Mike Bickle, the director of the International House of Prayer in Kansas City, defines strongholds this way: "A stronghold in the mind is a spiritual fortress made of wrong thoughts, a fortified dwelling place where demonic forces can hide and operate in power against us. The ideas and thoughts that make up the stronghold are based on lies that challenge the truth of what God has revealed about Himself."[2] That is very true, but they are also based on lies we believe about ourselves, especially in relation to God.

I would guess that most of us wrestle against dozens of lies, maybe even hundreds, depending on our own particular story. But for all of us, the lies we believe that come in conjunction with our major hurts and wounds—especially the ones we experience early on in life—are the lies that the devil builds his strongholds around. The earlier the experience and the bigger the hurt, the more easily it becomes part of your foundation. And then you have all of your subsequent hurts and wounds to reinforce that fortress, until it becomes impenetrable and feels like it's just a part of who you are. That makes it hard to identify strongholds on your own, and even harder to do anything about them by yourself. And if your strongholds involve people and relationships and you actually *need people and relationships* to tear them down ... well, that becomes a real challenge. Those strongholds usually end up getting buried deep in there, where most of us don't like to look. Sort of like the closets you throw all the junk in when company is coming over and you don't want anyone to see how disorganized you actually are! But this stuff isn't clutter, it's toxic and corrosive garbage (trash from the enemy's household!) and we *need* to get rid of it. Paul tells us,

> The weapons we fight with are not the weapons of the world. On the contrary, they have divine power to demolish strongholds. We demolish arguments and every pretension that sets itself up against the knowledge of God,

and we take captive every thought to make it obedient to Christ.

—2 Corinthians 10:4–5 NIV

Strongholds can only be destroyed by the power of God, with His divine weaponry. But these are not secret weapons. God does not intend for us to walk into battle unarmed. He has given us what we need to not just remove strongholds, but to *demolish* them. What are these divine weapons? The armor of God! God gives us His armor to clothe ourselves with what will protect us and now defines who we are. With the armor, we are wearing our identity on the outside, so that others—especially the enemy—will recognize we belong to God:

- **The helmet of salvation**, to protect our heads: we know we are saved, redeemed, and given the mind of Christ through His death and resurrection.

- **The breastplate of righteousness**, to protect our hearts: we have been made clean and holy through the blood of Jesus, and we have become the dwelling place of God Himself.

- **The shoes fitted with the gospel of peace**, to equip and enable us: our feet have been properly outfitted to carry out His work, ready to run the race set before us with the message that God is good, that He loves us, and in Him we find our strength and rest.

- **The shield of faith**, our ultimate protection: we carry with us our belief that God is who He says He is, and we can cover ourselves or anyone else with the assurance that He alone is our strength and our shield.

- **The belt of truth**, to wrap around our most vulnerable areas: we protect ourselves knowing that God is the only source of Truth, and the Spirit of Truth lives inside us.

- **The sword of the Spirit, which is the Word of God:** we carry with us the only offensive weapon we need, and as the Word became flesh on our behalf, we also have now become vessels of the Living Word ourselves!

Now that we are properly outfitted for battle, we can go about tearing down our strongholds. But first we need to identify what our strongholds are, and usually this is not a solo project. Even with the help of the Holy Spirit, we are not objective enough to be able to see ourselves from the outside looking in, so it is often very difficult to identify our strongholds on our own, much less get rid of them. We need the help of trustworthy, godly, discerning prayer ministers, counselors, or pastors to help us identify them, so if you haven't done so already, this is the time to seek out one or two of those people.

Our strongholds can usually be traced back to some sort of a choice or decision we made (an inner vow) in conjunction with an experience of deep emotional pain—either that which was done to us, or that which we've brought upon others. For example, if your dad walked out on the family, and you swore, "I'm never going to trust another man," or, when you failed a test at school and your parents came down really hard on you, you concluded, "I guess I'm just not good enough for anyone." Or, say you cheated on your girlfriend, causing her tremendous hurt, and you decided, "I am toxic to other people. I'm really just a jerk, when it comes down to it." When you look at these vows isolated in this way, they might not seem to be too big of a deal. But when those thoughts or feelings settle in your heart deeply, they begin to inform other thoughts, lead you to make judgments or conclusions that are inaccurate, and eventually they affect your decision-making, your actions, and larger and larger portions of your whole thought process. They become like cancerous cells that multiply and invade the healthy ones.

I'll give you my own personal example of a stronghold that fueled my orphan identity: "God, if you can't fix me, I'll find someone who will." Now, I never remember actually saying this to myself (or to God), and when I see it here in print, it really doesn't look all that bad. But, I'm telling you, this kind of a vow can—and did—have catastrophic results. For some people, that vow could lead them into serial relationships, trying to find *anyone* to fill the void; for others, it could create unattainable expectations within relationships, so that all of them would be doomed to fail. For me, it meant that any relationship that made me feel loved and valued had the potential to be the one that could fix me. And what if I ever found a relationship like that, and I lost it? I would be beyond help! I was able to stave off that scenario for a long time by not letting anyone become too close, too loved, or too important. Miraculously, my husband (who deserves sainthood!) was able to withstand my fears and testing until I was able to fully trust him and let him in. With time and healing, I was able eventually to let a few others into my heart in a very deep way. But as time went on, more and more of my identity became dependent on being loved and valued by those people. Of course, I did not realize that … until I lost them. And when I experienced that series of significant losses in a very short period of time, my worst fear overtook me. Of course, I was not actually "beyond help," but I believed it with my whole heart, because by that point my whole heart was functioning completely out of an orphan identity.

What are the lies you are believing? If any come to mind, it would be very helpful to write them down now. Then, when you are able to pray with someone about those lies, you need to start tracing them back to the point at which you first began believing them, noting the circumstances that led you to believe the lies in the first place. It may take some time and some digging, but you should be able to trace those lies back to some kind of vow you made as a result of something that hurt you, caused you fear, shame, doubt, regret, or whatever fits your particular situation. That's your stronghold, and of course you may uncover more than one. Digging around in garbage is messy, uncomfortable, and isn't fun, but don't get discouraged or overwhelmed—remember, it is necessary to clean everything out in order to get down to the old foundation. Once you've identified your strongholds, tearing them down is a fairly simple (though not necessarily easy) process:

- First, you need to come out of agreement with those lies and break the vow. You need to *reject, out loud, whatever vows you've made and lies you believed.*

- Second, you need to *ask the Lord for forgiveness for believing those lies* instead of His truth.

- Next, you need to *counter those lies with the truth of God as it is written in His Word.* For example, "*I reject the lie* that I am worthless, and I come out of agreement with the vow I made that I will never ask for anything. *I choose to believe the truth* that God says, 'I am fearfully and wonderfully made, and that I can ask for anything in His name and He will give it to me.'"

- Finally, once you've gone home from your ministry time, you will need to *reject the lies and speak the truths over yourself regularly* until you know the truths have taken root in your heart. This is how we become "transformed by the renewing of [our] minds."

Piece of cake, right? I know this stuff isn't easy, believe me. The truth is, it takes courage, faith, and determination to stare down your worst stuff and face it head on. But to use the household analogy again, cleaning out the basement (or garage, or attic) is hard work—sometimes tedious, discouraging, and overwhelming, maybe even frightening—but once it's all cleaned and organized, you feel so much better! And you have a sense of accomplishment. Tearing down strongholds is similar in that way; the rewards you will receive for all your hard work are huge: freedom from bondage to those lies, and freedom to be able to move on to even deeper, greater levels of freedom! And you must never forget that you have a Helper who works alongside you and *in you*, and He is both willing and able to put all that trash where it belongs … at the foot of the Cross.

#2: Sacrifices (and Offerings)

Once we have demolished our strongholds, Paul instructs us to take every thought captive and make it obedient to Christ. That sounds easy enough until you try to do it! The problem most of us encounter is that in order to do that, we have to give up control. I personally don't know anyone who doesn't have at least a few issues with control. I certainly do. With me, it's not that I'm particularly controlling in my behavior, but what goes on inside my head is a whole other matter! I am a professional worrier, and guess what? *Worry equals control.* And this is why: the thing that drives the need to control is fear. We want to gain control, be in control, and stay in control—all because we are afraid of what will happen if we're not.

Are you afraid to fly? I used to be. If you talk to people who are afraid to fly, most of them will tell you they cannot relax at all during the flight; they can't sleep, they can't watch movies or read, because they need to use all their mental energy to help the pilot fly the plane with their thoughts. Seriously! It's silly, but it's true. I know I do the very same thing with God: I don't have the basic trust in Him to turn over the things I worry about or fear, so I try to do His job for Him by controlling. It doesn't work at all.

Learning to trust God can be a painful process; it is a costly sacrifice to relinquish our control, even if being in control is only a perception. I remember mulling over the phrase *a costly sacrifice*, and then it dawned on me: *I can do that. I can sacrifice because I love Him.* One day the Lord showed me a vision. He took me through this picture of myself putting my control in a basket and laying it on His altar. Then I placed my meager offering of trust at the foot of His altar. The control was consumed by His fire—instantly gone, taken unto Him; but He took my trust and breathed on it, and it grew and came back to me. Do you remember what we said earlier about the Spirit as *breath*? When He breathed on it, I think what He was showing me was the Father adding the work of the Holy Spirit to my trust. He's the Helper, helping me to trust Him more. This was an exercise He led me to do every day for quite a while;

this was my process of taking my thoughts captive and making them obedient to Christ.

It is very important that the beginning steps on this journey are taken with much intentionality. It doesn't matter as much that you follow the exercise I've described exactly, but it does matter that, after you've torn down your strongholds, you begin the process of transforming and renewing your mind. Replace those lies with the truth, and then learn to allow the Lord to inform and shape your thought life. Jesus warned us about what will happen if we remove the demonic from our lives without filling the void with the kingdom of God:

> "When a defiling evil spirit is expelled from someone, it drifts along through the desert looking for an oasis, some unsuspecting soul it can bedevil. When it doesn't find anyone, it says, 'I'll go back to my old haunt.' On return it finds the person spotlessly clean, but vacant. It then runs out and rounds up seven other spirits more evil than itself and they all move in, whooping it up. That person ends up far worse off than if he'd never gotten cleaned up in the first place. That's what this generation is like: You may think you have cleaned out the junk from your lives and gotten ready for God, but you weren't hospitable to my kingdom message, and now all the devils are moving back in."

> —Matthew 12:43–45 MSG

Turning over my thought life to Jesus and asking Him to take charge of it has been one of the most difficult and, honestly, annoying steps in my journey. It's annoying how easily I fall back into destructive thought patterns! I still have to consciously redirect my thoughts to Him all the time; the difference now is I don't let them get quite as far as they used to before I realize what I need to do.

When I was a little girl, I had a scary and memorable incident riding my aunt's horse. My aunt had been sick and hadn't been able to exercise her horse in a couple of weeks, and the day I came to ride was the first day the horse had gotten to stretch its legs and run around. I'm sure it sensed I was not an experienced rider, so after a few minutes of trotting around the corral, the horse suddenly broke into a full gallop, and nothing I could do would stop that horse from running with all its might where it wanted to go. That's often how my thought life feels—like I'm on a runaway horse going wherever it pleases. As I've learned to take my thoughts captive and make them obedient to Christ, it has been like putting a bridle on that horse and teaching it (sometimes forcefully!) to go where *I* want it to go. And that's toward Jesus. Each time, every time, for the rest of my life—and that's the next step in our process.

#3 SANCTIFICATION

Sanctification is the process of submitting all of ourselves to becoming more holy, aligning every part of our lives with the Father's heart and purpose for us, so that we become more and more like Jesus. Obviously, that is not something we can do by our own strength, or something we can attain fully this side of heaven, but I think that is precisely what God had in mind:

> Remember, dear brothers and sisters, that few of you were wise in the world's eyes or powerful or wealthy when God called you. Instead, God chose things the world

considers foolish in order to shame those who think they are wise. And he chose things that are powerless to shame those who are powerful. God chose things despised by the world, things counted as nothing at all, and used them to bring to nothing what the world considers important. As a result, no one can ever boast in the presence of God. God has united you with Christ Jesus. For our benefit God made him to be wisdom itself. Christ made us right with God; he made us pure and holy [sanctified], and he freed us from sin. Therefore, as the Scriptures say, "If you want to boast, boast only about the Lord."

—1 Corinthians 1:26–31 NLT

What the Father has in mind for us is complete dependence on Him—that is why He gives us so many impossible commands! He tells us to do completely impossible things because *with God all things are possible*! By drawing us into total reliance on Him for everything we need, He not only accomplishes the impossible for us, but He does it through us—He allows us to partner with Him and be the conduits for miraculous things! In this His intention to make us dependent on Him isn't to make us slaves; it is to empower us to experience victory, freedom, blessing, and success in ways that just aren't attainable by our own strength.

Dependence on Him doesn't look like a wishy-washy, weakling kind of dependence, but it's the "heartbeats and breathing in sync" kind of dependence I wrote about in the first chapter. With God, dependence looks and feels like intimacy. To others, our dependence on Him can look foolish or weak, but what Paul is saying in the Scripture above is that our godliness, honed by our sanctification process through Christ, will "put them to shame" if they think they are the ones who are wise, powerful, and important.

You may be thinking, *Wait, I thought shame was supposed to be bad!* Yes … and no. Shame, when it's directed at us by others, by Satan, or by ourselves, is used to tear us down; it is destructive in nature and usually revolves around some sort of a lie. Shame used by God has an entirely different purpose—it comes as an awareness of a truth we're not seeing, a conviction of sinfulness, with the purpose of inspiring us to repent and come to the Father. The Holy Spirit can convict us of our sin by eliciting the feeling of shame within us. What Paul is teaching in that passage is that our righteousness will actually help others see their own sin, and if their hearts are receptive to His leading, it will draw them closer to the Lord. He uses our process of being made holy to call others to holiness, too.

What I have been learning is that sanctification not only involves our sin but also intends to engage every part of us, including our good qualities. I had the funny thought one day that every good quality in us seems to have an "evil twin"—that is, an unsanctified version of that good quality. Let's take generosity, for example. God tells us to be a cheerful giver and to be generous— with our time, with our money, with our resources. That's a good thing when it's submitted to the Lord. But think of how easily generosity can go wrong and be bad for us and for others. We can give irresponsibly, we can give out of wrong motives or priorities; our giving can cause others to be irresponsible or dependent or otherwise enable them in unhealthy behaviors or patterns. I think you get the picture. You can find all kinds of parallels in other gifts and strengths—our kindness, our honesty, our intelligence, our loving nature. Pretty much anything you pick. Sometimes we make good choices about how to steward those things and operate in them, and sometimes we do not. Sometimes it can go very, very wrong.

But this is why we need a Savior. If we truly want a victorious life, a life of freedom and wholeness, we cannot walk it out without walking out a process of sanctification with Jesus every day. When we give our hearts to Jesus and we're saved, we are washed clean and we are a new creation, but being that new creation, sanctified and holy, is not a one-time transaction, it is an ongoing process of dying to ourselves, kind of like the renewing of our minds. This is more than changing the way we think and submitting our thoughts to Christ. It is continually offering up all that we are and saying, "God, I want You to have all of me, and I'm not going to trust in my own abilities, my own strengths, or my own wisdom in how best to use them. I want You to teach me how to be the version of myself You had in mind when You created me."

My dad often mixes metaphors when he speaks; it's something I really love about him and it makes me smile when he does it. I've noticed that sometimes my heavenly Father does this, too, especially when He wants me to understand the lesson behind what He is teaching me. He did this for me during my season of extreme loss, to help me understand that even though He did not cause those losses, He would use them in my life to accomplish His purposes for me. I happened to have been reading about pruning in the book of John—you know, cutting off the dead branches or the ones not producing good fruit so the whole tree can produce better fruit. I began to pray about this, asking the Lord what branches in me needed to be pruned, and if there were other branches in my life (people or other things) that needed to be removed as well. God spoke to me and said, *"This is no pruning you are going through; it is a forest fire."* Picture that for a minute. The actual fire burning, ravaging, destroying. The heat, the chaos, the roar of the flames. And after the fire has gone through the whole forest and burned everything to the ground … utter destruction, desolation, scorched earth, complete emptiness. That's exactly what my life and my heart felt like. I wept at the thought of it. Then the Lord asked me, *"What happens after a forest fire?"* And the answer came to me: *new life, resurrection.* Later that night I decided to Google, "after a forest fire" and see what came up. The first thing that caught my eye was an article written by NASA called, "Evolving in the Presence of Fire." I love when God speaks to us like that! This is an excerpt from the article:

> Although most people regard fire as a destructive force that should be fought and quickly extinguished, the fact is the boreal forest evolved in the presence of fire and has adapted to it. … "Fire is the mechanism by which the forest is continually regenerated." … Fires consume dead, decaying vegetation accumulating on the forest floor, thereby clearing the way for new growth.[3]

I also read somewhere once that there are certain seeds that can only sprout and grow after they have been burned by fire. That's an amazing thought when you're facing a blackened, burned landscape all around you. Just because the Lord didn't cause the fire doesn't mean He won't use it for our good. He does. His fire brings about purification, sanctification, refinement:

> "I will bring that group through the fire
> and make them pure.
> I will refine them like silver

and purify them like gold.
They will call on my name,
and I will answer them.
I will say, 'These are my people,'
and they will say, 'The LORD is our God.'"

—Zechariah 13:9 NLT

New growth, new life, resurrection life. He promises this to us when we go through the fire and as we go about the process of sanctification. He brings the new and the resurrected into our lives not just once when we are saved, but throughout our lives and in any situation where we need to look more like Jesus. Sanctification brings about resurrection life, and that is life infused with the supernatural, making us look like Jesus—like true sons and daughters.

#4: SURRENDER

This one was (and is) a tough one for me. What comes immediately to my mind when I see this word is probably the first time I ever saw it in print. It was that ominous scene in the *Wizard of Oz*, when Dorothy and her friends look to the sky to see what the Wicked Witch of the West has written in black smoke: *Surrender Dorothy*. It makes me shudder when I think about it. Then I learned more about "surrender" in history class, in relation to the many battles and wars that everyone studies about in school. I have this association with it of ultimate impending doom, that sickening moment you know all is lost.

But when it comes to our relationship with the Father, that association simply is not accurate. It's not even an accurate definition of the word, not in its complete meaning and usage, anyway. In relation to God, *surrender* means "yieldedness." It's very similar to sacrificing control and giving ourselves as an offering, but, in my opinion, surrendering goes even deeper than that. It's like turning over the very essence of who we are to the Lord. That feels pretty frightening to me. Yet if we want our orphan hearts to be free to receive the Father's love and be able to accept our adoption by Him, we must do just that:

> Simply start by admitting that you cannot cure yourself. You have to say yes fully to your powerlessness in order to let God heal you. But it is not really a question of *first* and *then*. Your willingness to experience your powerlessness already includes the beginning of surrender to God's action in you. When you cannot sense anything of God's healing presence, the acknowledgement of your powerlessness is too frightening. It's like jumping from a high wire without a net to catch you.

> Your willingness to let go of your desire to control your life reveals a certain trust. The more you relinquish your stubborn need to maintain your power, the more you will get in touch with the One who has the power to heal and guide you. And the more you get in touch with that divine power, the easier it will be to confess to yourself and others your basic powerlessness.

—Henri J. M. Nouwen, *The Inner Voice of Love*[4]

I read *The Inner Voice of Love* during the darkest period of that season of loss, and I felt like the author had a window to my very soul. In fact, throughout that whole season I read so many of Nouwen's books, he began to feel like a personal friend and guide through my adoption process. I highly recommend reading some of his books, if you can. In some ways, surrendering ourselves to the Lord is very much an act of will—we have to choose to do it. Our orphan-hearted independent streak runs contrary to doing this, so it hardly comes naturally. But as much as it is a choice and an act of will, it is also something we need God's help with to allow it to happen. Like Nouwen said, no one wants to jump from a high wire without a net—and though we can decide to trust God, trust is something that has to be built and won by experience.

We can begin surrendering ourselves to God by asking Him to help build our trust; to show us if we let go a little bit, He will be there to catch us before we fall too far. There is a lyric I love from a song I have been singing lately, "Grace So Glorious," by Elevation Worship: *Oh, the glory of the Savior's love surrounding our surrender.*[5] I love that picture! There is little else that makes us feel as naked and vulnerable as surrendering our whole selves, our will, to One we cannot even see. But in His mercy and lovingkindness, Jesus' love surrounds our surrender, so it is safe, covered, and protected. We can't surrender all the way (everything) in one shot, the first time we decide to (at least, that has not been my experience); each time it's a little bit more, a little bit more. I described it to a friend once as gently prying one finger at a time open from what we are clinging to, until at last we are left with open hands. And it is when we are able to have open hands that we are truly able to receive.

My son, give me your heart, and let your eyes observe
my ways.

—Proverbs 23:26

So, there we have our Four S's: *Strongholds, Sacrifice, Sanctification,* and *Surrender.* Like I said, I have never been one to ease in to things! This is all pretty big, pretty difficult stuff. But these things are so critical to attend to if we sincerely want to get down to that old foundation and replace it with a new one. It is not at all necessary to do these four things sequentially in the order I wrote them, nor are they steps that must be completed in their entirety before you move on to the other steps I will outline in subsequent chapters. We are all unique individuals, and our processes should reflect that. I do know these things are necessary, though, in the process of teaching our orphan hearts about their adoption by the Father.

As illustration, let me share a little adoption parallel from an experience within my own family. My children do not need to earn their sonship by their behavior—they have already been adopted, and that's a fact. We love them unconditionally, and that is a fact. But it's also a fact that our newly adopted children still have orphan hearts even as they relate to us on a day-to-day basis. There are many ways we are trying to teach them what it means to be a son and daughter, and many different tactics we use to help them learn it. The first six months they were with us, our kids continued to call us "aunt" and "uncle" as they had in Uganda, which was a title of respect. But it was also a refusal to call us "Mom" and "Dad." They also refused to hug us anymore, though they did so freely back at the orphanage. These two things were crucial for them to do if they were ever going to be able to look and act like a true son and daughter. So … we made them. They had to call us Mom and Dad and, at the very least, give us a hug at bedtime, or they would incur some negative consequence. I'm sure they would tell you themselves how much they hated that process, how difficult it was for them to surrender their own will and do what we were asking them to. It was definitely a fake-it-'til-you-make-it process. But sometimes that is exactly what we need to do. The good thing is, in this case, it isn't just pretending. Acting the way a son or daughter acts serves as both the tool and the process of it becoming genuine. So it is with the Four S's. They are extremely important "tools" or steps toward the goal of helping your orphan heart embrace its adoption, but doing those things—tearing down strongholds with the armor of God, sacrificing control or other things we'd rather hold on to, submitting all of ourselves to the process of sanctification, and surrendering our will and our entire being to the Father—are what true sons and daughters do, how true sons and daughters act, and what true sons and daughters look like.

Our Father in heaven is exceedingly more patient and loving than we are as parents. He never lets frustration or exasperation cloud His judgment, He never withholds His love. He never entertains thoughts of giving up on us because it's too difficult. Every step we take toward claiming our sonship, no matter how small or tentative, is celebrated and blessed by the Father. He will cheer us on and give us all we need to keep going on the journey— He just wants us to keep going. I do, too. Keep walking, don't get discouraged, don't give up. No turning back now; we're on our way.

Boldly

Boldly, God, I can approach Your throne;
humbly, God, for I know who You are:
King of the Universe, the Mighty One surrounded by heavenly beings
of Your own creation,
day and night, they only live to praise Your name.

Enthroned in majesty, He would be untouchable if it were not for His love.
For His love exceeds the limitless bounds of His terrifying power,
it goes deeper than the bottomless chasm of His mercy and grace.
His kindness no one can fathom.

This Great King, the Master and Maker of all—He is my Father
and I have captured His heart.
His eye is fixed on me always,
His watchful, protective, loving gaze never wanders.
I am the apple of His eye; He is forever taken with me.
I am his little girl.

CHAPTER 8

Pledge Your Allegiance

The child asks of the Father whom he knows. Thus, the essence of Christian prayer is not general adoration, but definite, concrete petition. The right way to approach God is to stretch out our hands and ask of One who we know has the heart of a Father.

—Dietrich Bonhoeffer[1]

In October 2012, we all stood in the judge's chambers in Uganda. We were told by our lawyer a day earlier, "This is a family court; you should expect a family atmosphere. It will be relaxed and friendly." Standing there in that room, I can assure you it was anything but friendly. The judge was intimidating and the atmosphere was tense and foreboding. We were there to petition for guardianship of our children—Uganda does not allow foreigners to complete the legal adoption there, but you may be granted legal guardianship and then take the children back to your home country to adopt them. So there we were: me, my husband, one of our daughters, our two "prospective children," two representatives from the orphanage, our lawyer, the judge, and the children's parents. Even though the kids had been abandoned years ago, it was required that both parents be present at the hearing because they are still living. Their presence, along with their signatures, represented their consent to the adoption of the children. I thought that was all that would be needed. To our surprise, the judge called our twelve-year-old new daughter up to the microphone to ask her some questions. She had to testify for herself and on behalf of her brother that they both wanted to be adopted. The judge asked her if she recognized her mother and her father sitting there in the room, and then asked her to testify in front of everyone present that she chose to have us as her parents in place of her natural parents. It struck me how much courage it must have taken for her to do this.

WHO (OR WHAT) IS SITTING IN THE FATHER'S SEAT?

The Lord brought this story to mind during my healing process to teach me something very powerful, and I want to share it with you as an important next step in the journey. What He showed me was very symbolic, so hang in there with me as I try to explain. To begin with, my prayers often went something like this: *God, You know how much I want to know You as Father. I want to feel like You're my Father and I'm Your daughter, and I want to be able to feel Your love. I want You to be all I need and I want to be able to find my identity and security in You. For some reason, I just can't ... and I don't know why.* One day as I was praying, the Lord gave me a startling response. He brought to mind the story of our kids in the judge's chambers and called my attention to the fact that Victoria had to decide to break ties with her parents and choose to be adopted by us. She couldn't come under our parentage if she still belonged to other parents. I immediately understood what the Lord was getting at; He was not able to take His place as Father in my heart because that place was already occupied. The question I heard next in my spirit was this: *"What are the things you're allowing to parent you, instead of Me?"*

And that is the question I want to pose to you.

I am not saying we need to cut ties with our natural parents in order to claim our adoption by the Father—not really, anyway, but I'll get to that later. What I am referring to now is that our earthly parents are supposed to provide and define for us love, acceptance, nurture, comfort, praise, value, and identity while we are children in their care. According to God's perfect design, we should receive those things from our parents, and our parents would then teach us to seek and receive them from the Father. That's in a perfect world, but none of us were raised in a perfect world. Whether we have received those things from our parents in part or not at all, we were made to need them. Whenever we are *not* seeking and receiving love, acceptance, nurture, comfort, praise, value, or identity from the Father, *we will seek it somewhere else*. And whatever gives us any of those things instead essentially becomes a parent to us.

So then, what are the things that are occupying the Father's seat in your heart? What gives you the ultimate love and acceptance you crave? Very often it's a person or people. It could be parental figures, a friend, your spouse—even your kids! Naturally, there is nothing wrong with receiving love and acceptance from others, even with allowing others to help you discover your identity. What becomes an issue is when a person or other people become your *primary, foundational source* of love, acceptance, value, and identity.

Since the Lord uses people to show His love and minister acceptance, healing, and a whole host of other good things, it can be hard to recognize at first when we have allowed one person or multiple people to take God's place. And while people are great to receive immediate in-the-flesh love, affection, and attention, eventually what you receive from them will begin to feel hollow if the Lord Himself isn't the primary source. That sense of hollowness is a setup for all kinds of unhealthy relationships and behaviors lying under the surface and gnawing at you until you are left trying to fill it some other way.

Which leads to another question: What do you seek out to nurture you or give you comfort? You know, the things you turn to when things get really difficult and stressful, or when you experience fear, shame, loneliness, or restlessness—things like food, alcohol, drugs, or other addictive substances and behaviors. But deep down we all know those things do not provide us true comfort; they just alleviate the *dis*comfort temporarily, as sociologist and author Brené Brown describes here:

> We create a dangerous cycle. We are the most in-debt, obese, addicted, and medicated people in US history – all because we try to numb our feelings of vulnerability. Unfortunately, we cannot selectively numb certain uncomfortable emotions. We end up numbing everything, including joy, gratitude and happiness. Then we're miserable, looking for purpose and meaning … and choose to numb again.[2]

I've always had the hunch that if I could just run into the Father's arms and let them close around me, those uncomfortable feelings and emotions would just go away. The truth is, they probably would! But before I even let my heart hope for that, it just seems easier and more immediately gratifying to try to alleviate them myself. Then I'm stuck in that cycle described above. Think of children who run to a parent for comfort when they get hurt, angry, or bored, but instead of helping the children deal with their feelings head on, Mom or Dad offers something like food or TV to calm the child down. When those kids eventually grow up, food or TV becomes the parent they run to when they experience negative feelings. I think on some level we all experience this.

Where do we get our value and our sense of worth? I heard once that we all have an essential question that burns within our souls. For men, it is, *Am I good enough?* And for women, it is, *Am I worthy to be loved?* I don't know if that strikes a chord in you, but it sure did in me when I heard it. We all need so desperately to know that our lives have meaning and that we have unique and irreplaceable value. So we search for someone or something to define us, to provide measurement, something we can point to and claim, "See? *That* shows that I am somebody." We choose good things by which we can measure ourselves, of course: good people, success, achievement, charity, talents, even our hobbies. Because these things are good in and of themselves and they make us feel good and valuable in light of them, it can be hard to see that measuring our value by them is a trap. The trap is the mere fact that everything on earth that has the potential to make us feel valuable is impermanent, unstable, and susceptible to brokenness and sin. So if your value and worth are tied to any one of those things, and you lose your amazing job, your charity goes under, you age out of being the athlete you once were, or your mentor turns his back on you, well, who are you *now*?

I think it's safe to say we look to all of these things on some level, much of the time. It's in our orphan nature to do so. Some of us are more reliant on some things than others, and many of us are probably in the dark as to how much or how often we are. I know I've read about and heard sermons on "What sits on the throne in your life?" Most often I've equated that question with issues with authority, as in, *Is God really God in your life?* I would always think, *Of course He is.* That is probably why the Lord Himself rephrased it to me in terms of what I'm allowing to parent me. The question addresses more than just who the authority figure is in my life. It also asks who or what has my affection most, what voice do I listen to first and above all else, where do I run for comfort, safety, and reassurance, and what ultimately defines me and gives me value? If I am being honest, I have concluded, *Everything else but God.*

So now what? All of this was a very sobering realization for me, and maybe it is for you, too. If we truly love the Lord, it should make us sad and even ashamed that, with all we know and have been taught, we've done it again—we've turned to other gods instead of God. But this is hardly a new or surprising pattern; we know that and God knows that. Mercifully, He has not left us helpless or hopeless to remain stuck in our patterns but has given us divine patterns to restore and overcome (*He is the cure!*). Much of what we need to employ is described in the previous chapter, such as breaking strongholds and learning to surrender ourselves fully to God. Now we can take what we have learned thus far and apply it to the process of breaking ties with the things we've allowed to parent us, and allowing God to take His rightful place as Father in our hearts.

A Word About Our "Real" Parents

Children, obey your parents; this is the right thing to
do because God has placed them in authority over you.
Honor your father and mother. This is the first of God's
Ten Commandments that ends with a promise. And this
is the promise: that if you honor your father and mother,
yours will be a long life, full of blessing.

—Ephesians 6:1–3 TLB

I want to talk now about our parents. Not the things we use
as substitutes, but the real ones: your biological parents, whether
they've both raised you or not, and your adoptive parents, if you
have them. First and foremost, we are told to honor them. You
know something is important to God if He makes it one of the Ten
Commandments, and even more important if He also attached a
promise to it! But there are no further qualifiers attached to that
commandment. He does not say to honor them *if* they were good
parents, *if* they were there for you, *if* they were godly people, *if*
you actually knew them at all … He just says to honor them. So,
what does it mean to honor them, and how do you do that? At
minimum, I think that honoring our parents means holding regard
and respect for their position as the ones who brought us into the
world. With healthier relationships, it means a certain amount of
reverence and devotion for who they are and what they've done
for us. Naturally, there is no one-size-fits-all formula for carrying
out this commandment, so we each must seek the Lord for the
specifics that fit our particular parents in our unique situations. If
your relationship with them is healthy, it should be fairly easy. If it's
unhealthy (to whatever degree), or if you did not know one or both

of them, honoring them becomes a challenge. Like I said earlier, God requires some impossible things of us, but His supernatural help makes them all possible. It can be done. The simplest, easiest thing we can honor our parents for is for giving us life. Whether you were planned or not, celebrated or not, or even raised by them or not, you are here by their biological help. We may not know or understand any more than that very basic information, but we can still confess and profess honor before God and others that our parents gave us life. This is what we have taught our adopted children, and we hope one day that they may even be able to extend that honor directly to their biological parents. Beyond that fundamental basis for honor, there are other things and other ways to honor your parents in less than ideal circumstances. If honoring either or both of your parents is difficult for you to do, there are some specific things you can do to position yourself to honor them before the Lord:

- Forgive them for where they have fallen short. Every parent has disappointed their child in some way; every one of us has been hurt by them at one time or other. Some parents have done egregious things to their children, and forgiving them does not mean any of those things were okay. But we are told to forgive or we won't be forgiven ourselves. However long it takes, we must work through a process of forgiving our parents until we know we have released all offenses to the Lord.

- Make a list of things you can genuinely thank the Lord for, for each of your parents. They may be small and seemingly unimportant things, but if those are the only things you can be thankful for, they can be counted as honor toward them.

- If you have a relationship with them, draw healthy boundaries between them and yourself (you may have to figure out what those are first—read *Boundaries* by Dr. Henry Cloud!). It is not honoring to be a doormat or to otherwise be responsible for filling every need and whim for them. Healthy boundaries are good for you and for them, even if it doesn't feel comfortable at first.

- Wherever you can show love and kindness with the Lord's help, do it. If it means picking just one thing to do or say to them regularly as a demonstration of honor, you can do it; the Lord will help you if you ask Him. Dedicate that one thing to the Lord as a statement of honoring your parents.

- Ask the Lord for healing and restoration in your relationship with your parents, and in their lives individually. You may have to surrender your ideas of what that might look like, but believe the Lord will bring it about as you walk closely with Him and as you honor your mother and father.

These are just a few suggestions, but they are tried and tested ones. The key is asking for the Holy Spirit's help where you need it. There's no question that God wants us to honor our parents; we may just need to ask Him for help doing it. And the promise attached to the commandment is there for us—He will bless our lives for our obedience.

Next, I want to talk about "breaking ties" with our parents, but I certainly don't mean that in the literal sense—only when there is danger arising from severe dysfunction should we actually permanently break relationship with our parents. Nevertheless, some of us remain overly connected to our parents even when we reach adulthood, and it is very common for grown adults to continue to define themselves by what their parents think of them, gauge their value and worth by how proud they make them, and seek to please them and gain their approval above all other relationships. This can occur within good relationships as well as in bad ones, and we can be completely oblivious to the fact that we are functioning this way. Some people are unconsciously still striving to live up to their parents' expectations, even after they have passed away. There is also the common tendency to unconsciously project characteristics of our parents (and the way we feel about them) onto Father God. Some of us view God as aloof and distant, some see Him as authoritarian and punishing. Maybe others even see Him as being weak and impotent. Whatever the characteristic may be, most of us unknowingly transfer some of what we experience from our parents onto God and our relationship with Him.

It's in these types of situations—being overly connected and projecting—that we need to symbolically and spiritually cut those ties with our parents. We need to break the ties between our parents and ourselves, and also the ones we may have created between our parents and God. You know the phrase, "cutting the cord," that people use when they see someone overly connected to their parents? It's basically just like that. In addition to that, I think it's also a great idea to ask the Lord to "grow a cord" (like an umbilical cord) between Him and us. A friend prayed that over me once—an umbilical cord connecting God to me—and it was a very powerful image. That cord became my lifeline. I want to be so connected to God that it's like a mother and her unborn child; I want to be the child whose life and everything she needs comes from the One I'm connected to. I believe the Father desires the same thing.

ALLOWING THE FATHER TO TAKE HIS SEAT

Hopefully, I've given you some things to consider and some steps to take in making room in your heart for the Father. Unhealthy projections or connections with your parents, not honoring them as you should, or allowing other things and people to parent you in ways only the Father can—all these contribute to crowding out the only One who deserves to be seated in the highest place of honor in your heart and life. It would be good to make a list of these things and systematically bring them before the Lord in prayer, either alone or with a prayer partner. It has been a comfort to me in my own process to know that there are concrete things such as these that I can do to get farther down the road to my goal. In fact, when I first realized (through the Holy Spirit's help) what I had allowed, I was pretty excited because I knew, in this case, there was something I could actually do about it! We've talked quite a bit about the Father's heart, but I want to look at some Scripture passages that describe Father God in the parenting role, the One who ultimately gives us love, acceptance, nurture, comfort, praise, value, and identity.

Do you remember the poem "Footprints in the Sand" by Mary Stevenson? I think most of us have come across this poem in some form—on a greeting card, poster, or T-shirt—with a beautiful beach scene in the background and two pairs of footprints in the sand. It talks about a dream the author had of walking on the beach with the Lord. It is a wonderful encouragement and reminder to us that God never leaves us, especially in times of trouble, and that often He carries us through those hard times rather than walking beside us. I'm not sure whether it was an actual dream the author had, but I do know the truth and even the imagery of this poem comes right from Scripture:

> The LORD your God who goes before you will himself fight for you, just as he did for you in Egypt before your eyes, and in the wilderness, where you have seen how the LORD your God carried you, as a man carries his son, all the way that you went until you came to this place.

—Deuteronomy 1:30–31

This is the original "Footprints in the Sand" story; though not set on a beach by the ocean, but in the desert, as the Israelites wandered through the Sinai from Egypt on their way to the promised land. When I first came across this verse it touched me deeply—no matter what translation you look at, all describe God carrying His people as a father carries a son. Picture that image for a moment: a boy, up on his dad's shoulders, arms around his neck; the father and son happily chatting as they walk along; the father pointing out things for the son to see. From this vantage point, the son can see from the father's perspective, and the world doesn't look as scary and overwhelming from there. As the boy begins to doze off, the father lifts him down from his shoulders and cradles him in his arms, and while the son sleeps, the father keeps watch and carries him on.

In Isaiah 66, the Lord prophesies to Isaiah about the future (and final) restoration of Israel, and He compares Jerusalem to a mother nursing her children and bouncing them on her knee. It paints a picture for us that one day we will find all we need within the Lord's Holy City; there and then we will be truly satisfied. God Himself promises, *"I will comfort you there as a little one is comforted by its mother"* (v. 13 TLB). The Lord is using incredibly intimate and familial language here to show us just how loving and nurturing He really is. Again, He says:

> "Listen to me, O house of Jacob,
> all the remnant of the house of Israel,
> who have been *borne by me from before your birth,*
> *carried from the womb;*
> even to your old age I am he,
> *and to gray hairs I will carry you.*
> I have made, and I will bear;
> *I will carry* and will save."
>
> —Isaiah 46:3–4

He carries us. Like a father, like a mother, but also like no parent anyone has ever experienced. He *wants* to carry us, from cradle to grave and throughout eternity. Great and Majestic as He is, He wants to bend down and scoop us up into His loving arms; and when we are with Him, we are never too old to be carried. The gentleness and tenderness of God is so overwhelming in these verses—He is showing us that He is and wants to be our source of true comfort and nurture, love, and affection.

Lastly, what about our value and worth? What does God say about that? Hear the Father whisper these words into your orphan heart:

> "Don't be afraid, I've redeemed you.
> I've called your name. You're mine.
> When you're in over your head, I'll be there with you.

When you're in rough waters, you will not go down.
When you're between a rock and a hard place,
it won't be a dead end—
Because I am GOD, your personal God,
The Holy of Israel, your Savior.
I paid a huge price for you:
all of Egypt, with rich Cush and Seba thrown in!
That's how much you mean to me!
That's how much I love you!
I'd sell off the whole world to get you back,
trade the creation just for you.

"So don't be afraid: I'm with you.
I'll round up all your scattered children,
pull them in from east and west.
I'll send orders north and south:
'Send them back.
Return my sons from distant lands,
my daughters from faraway places.
I want them back, every last one who bears my name,
every man, woman, and child
Whom I created for my glory,
yes, personally formed and made each one.'"

—Isaiah 43:2–7 MSG

For thus says the LORD of hosts: "He sent Me after glory, to the nations which plunder you; for *he who touches you touches the apple of His eye.*"

—Zechariah 2:8 NKJV

"Can a mother forget the baby at her breast
and have no compassion on the child she has borne?
Though she may forget,
I will not forget you!
See, I have engraved you on the palms of my hands;
your walls are ever before me."

—Isaiah 49:15–16 NIV

For me, believing my value and worth to God at a heart level has been very difficult. I'm not really sure why, and it is something about which I continue to seek His wisdom, so I can get down to the original root lie, remove it, and then replace it with the truth. Until then (and forever afterward), I find it helpful to read verses such as the ones written above. Sometimes, I'll even imagine my name written or spoken before them, as if the Father is saying these things directly to me—because He is! I have also found it really helpful to read the verses I'm reflecting on in different translations (www.biblegateway.com is a great resource) because sometimes a particular wording will speak to my heart in a way that sort of "catches" and allows it to sink in. Although I do believe it is best to be able to get at the root of things that block our hearts from receiving what the Father has for us, sometimes the way to get at that root is to keep rehearsing the truths over and over, letting them sink down until they displace the lie that sits at the bottom. It may be that over time the lie surfaces on its own, without digging around for it, and if and when it does, we can tend to it the same way we do when we uncover our strongholds.

Finally, a few words about our identity through the Father: You can read and listen to volumes about it in books and sermons, and of course in the Bible. You'll find this topic everywhere, because there are so many orphans longing to know their identities! From everything I have learned and experienced, I can say with confidence that we all need to regularly rehearse the truth of who we are. There are many great resources out there that will help you list truths about your identity. Write those truths in your journal, copy them on Post-it® Notes and stick them on your bathroom mirror or the fridge, have them with you at your desk—anyplace you pass often enough to remind yourself. I've added my own list below, based on those passages from Isaiah and Zechariah. I suggest writing your own name in the spaces provided:

- *You,* _____, are the one the Father carries— on His shoulders, in His arms, through difficult seasons when you need His help.

- *You,* _____, are the one who can run to Him anytime you want to for comfort, and He will scoop you up in His arms with a mother's love.

- The Father carried *you,* _____, in His heart before you were even conceived; He carried *you* along with your mother, in the womb as you developed. From the time you were born, until the time you are old and gray, *you are the one* the Lord delights to carry.

- *You,* _____, belong to the Father—He has called *you* by name.

- *You,* _____, are the one for whom He would go anywhere and do anything to save!

- The Father would trade all of creation for *you,*

_____, in order to have you with Him, where you belong.

- *You,* _____, are the apple of His eye!

- *You,* _____, are the one He loves so dearly, like a mother who nurses you at her breast. As great a picture of love that is, He loves *you* more!

- *Your name,* _____, is written on His hands; the hands that are always at work, always before Him. *Your name* never passes out of the forefront of His mind!

See what great love the Father has lavished on us, that we should be called children of God! And that is what we are! (1 John 3:1 NIV). We are *His*, beloved friends. We belong to Him and He belongs to us. What He gives, nothing and no one can give. He is the *only thing* that can satisfy the longings of our souls. He is the *only cure* for our orphan hearts. He is worthy of our love, our praise, our honor, and our *allegiance.* We must pledge our allegiance only to Him, and let all else fall into their proper places once we allow Him to take His rightful seat on the throne in our hearts. When we can say we have done this, we are nearly home.

Heart Wide Open

Here I sit before you, having run an uncharted course;
sometimes tentatively edging around the perimeter,
sometimes, for fear, turning to bolt in the other direction.
But always, always I am drawn to my destination—to sit before you.
And so I've run, breathless and trembling from casting aside
all my protective armor that keeps me safe from the outside world.
Because I know who you are, I want to be known by you.
Because I know who you are, I cannot be satisfied by half-truths
or projections of anything else that is not real.
If you only love the mask I put on, I will shrink back and die a little inside;
for the mask hides and perverts and corrupts
that which is pure and righteous and holy,
and renders real love invalid.
And so, for this all-or-nothing pursuit I have come
to sit before you;
defenseless, raw, open, vulnerable ...
wanting to be seen,
wanting to be known,
wanting to be loved—just as I am.

CHAPTER 9

Be Brave

I learned that courage was not the absence of fear, but the triumph over it. The brave man is not he who does not feel afraid, but he who conquers that fear.

—Nelson Mandela[1]

What does being brave have to do with being a true son or daughter of the King? Everything! Of course we are loved and adopted by Him regardless of our strengths and weaknesses, and certainly He won't love us any less if we are cowardly, but I believe being brave is a hallmark—an identifying characteristic—of being one of the Father's children. It takes a certain amount of bravery to push through the things that hold us back from living as children who have been grafted in, and it takes further bravery to authentically live from an identity firmly rooted in Christ. In this chapter, I want to devote some time and space to being brave in the Lord.

A Working Definition

I want to begin by defining what I think it means to be *brave in the Lord*. This is my own definition and you won't find it in the dictionary. Most dictionaries would tell you that *brave* means "fearless" or "without fear," but to me, that doesn't make sense. How can you be brave if you're not facing something you fear? And is there a certain standard of "brave," or is bravery in the eye of the beholder? I mean, getting on an airplane for a cross-country flight is hardly brave if you have no fear of flying. But if you do fear flying and you get on that plane anyway, that is brave, isn't it? So, for our purposes, let's throw out any notion that brave means being fearless and presenting a stiff upper lip in the face of danger; instead, let's think of being brave as *being willing to do what it takes to be an overcomer*, for the Bible says that "everyone born of God overcomes the world" (1 John 5:4 NIV).

We talked in the first chapter about fear being one of the four chambers of the orphan heart. We said that whatever we fear, we become subject to; fear makes us a slave. Each of us undoubtedly has a unique mix of things we fear, and they can range from things that can stop us in our tracks to things we merely avoid. That leads me to the first point I want to make about being brave in the Lord: We must stop avoiding the issues inside ourselves that are uncomfortable, inconvenient, and messy to face. I am convinced that many of us miss out on so many blessings, on so much growth and healing and freedom, because we are afraid to face our own junk. We're afraid of the time it might take, afraid of the feelings that might rise to the surface, and afraid to admit the truth that sometimes we're wrong or our thoughts are more dysfunctional than we own up to.

Or, what if we find out that one issue is linked to another, which is linked to yet another … and we might just have to tackle *all* of them? What if we're afraid to discover we are actually as bad inside as we suspect we are? There are lots of valid reasons to not want to take on this kind of a challenge, especially when we are still living like an orphan, determined to go it alone. But if we want—*really want*—to know God as Father and have that reality change our lives, we have to be willing to tackle the issues that keep us from it. I may have listed steps and suggestions on how to deal with strongholds, to learn how to sacrifice our control, and allow ourselves to get to a place of complete surrender to the Lord, but I am well aware that actually doing those things is not an easy task. You need courage just to begin, and then plenty of it when bigger and deeper fears start to surface. When pain and sadness surface, we all tend to go to great lengths to avoid them when we can. So it's only natural that we would want to avoid this whole messy process—it's full of stuff we don't like and are afraid of. But this is exactly where being *brave in the Lord* comes in.

We Are Bravehearted Children

There's an intriguing thing about courage: The root word comes from the Latin word *cor*, which means "heart." Courage literally begins from the heart. It makes sense, then, that the phrase *take heart* generally means "be brave" or "be courageous." Immediately this quote from Jesus comes to mind:

> "I have told you these things, so that in me you may

have peace. In this world you will have trouble. But take heart! I have overcome the world."

—John 16:33 NIV

If courage—being brave—comes from the heart and arises out of it, what "heart" are we talking about—the orphan heart? No! *The heart that has been grafted in.* It may seem a backwards process, being told to use something you are not yet in touch with. Yet our grafted-in heart was given to us when we first accepted Jesus as our Savior, and we can "call it into action" when we need to take on all that scary stuff. You don't need to feel like a son or daughter yet; you just need to choose to activate the renewed heart you've been given. It's very similar to putting on the armor of God—we can *put on*, or *activate*, our grafted-in heart when we're ready to face our hurts, our issues, and our strongholds. The grafted-in heart is needed to revisit and heal from memories that are painful, to forgive those who caused the really big hurts, and to inspire us to choose the things of the kingdom over the things of this world. We know already that we never take on these things alone—the Helper is always with us—but that doesn't mean it won't require courage on our part to get it started and get it done.

It took nearly five years of waiting before we could finally bring our Ugandan children home. We were initially granted permission to pursue their adoption by the director of their orphanage in 2008, but for a number of reasons, the pieces that needed to be in place to actually begin the legal process kept pushing the date further and further back, so we could not begin the real paperwork until the spring of 2012, and we were finally able to bring the children home on Thanksgiving weekend that same year. During that long waiting period, the Lord gave me a number of dreams; one of them in particular is a good illustration of what we're talking about here.

I was in Uganda with my family, and our two Ugandan children were with us. We were all at some kind of nature preserve, standing on a lookout platform and watching for animals. Out of the corner of my eye I saw a leopard (which I believe represented the devil) and recognized he was stalking Victoria. In the blink of an eye, she noticed, too, and took off running. I was screaming after her, "Don't run, Victoria, it will catch you! Come back to me!" But she was so terrified she just kept running. The leopard was gaining on her and all hope seemed lost. Then the Holy Spirit spoke to me (in my dream) and said, *Do it! Call it forth, speak it out loud—you know what you must say!* I knew what I was supposed to say, but I was afraid. But as the leopard got closer and closer and there was no time left, I screamed, "Victoria! Come to Mama!" She turned and looked at me and ran toward me. The dream ended.

There were two messages in that dream. One applied right then when I dreamed it, and one would be needed later on. I don't remember at what point in the five-year wait I had the dream, but I can tell you for sure I was losing hope the adoption would actually happen. The longer time went on, the further the children seemed to be slipping away from us. In the dream, I was afraid to call myself "Mama" because I was afraid to put that out there, to speak it out loud and then be bitterly disappointed if it didn't happen. I was also afraid (in the dream, and then later in real life) that if Victoria didn't acknowledge me as her mother, my heart would break with that rejection. I remember that dream so vividly I can still remember what it felt like, trying to summon all the courage I had to shout it out; I believe wholeheartedly that it required my courage (which was rooted in my faith) in order to overcome the spiritual opposition we were facing to the adoption. My proclaiming myself as her mother was a prophetic declaration that needed to happen to bring those children home. The other message in that dream was for Victoria—she needed to acknowledge me as her mother and allow herself to run to me for safety and protection, as a means of overcoming what the devil had planned for her. I can assure you that in real life it has taken Victoria much courage to do that. Every brave step she takes toward accepting us as her parents (and all that comes with it) brings her more healing, more wholeness, and more freedom.

We need to be bravehearted children when it comes to claiming our full sonship in the Lord. The Lord Himself never contests our adoption—it is freely given, and we must come to a place of being able to freely receive it. But we do need to claim it for ourselves, because we have an enemy of our souls who will do everything he can to contest and oppose it. Once you belong to Jesus, Satan cannot have you—but he can do everything in his power to make you ineffective as a Christian and lure you away from all the blessings and benefits of living as a true son or daughter of God. So we must be brave, we must overcome, and we must begin activating our grafted-in hearts.

True Bravery Is Borne From Faith

In order to be brave, one must be convinced that 1) there is a higher purpose that justifies the risk involved, 2) the potential gain is worth the risk of potential loss, and 3) there is something or someone to rely on to give us confidence that we can do what we're about to do. Real courage acknowledges that there are no guarantees of success, and being brave requires faith—faith in *something*, anyway. As believers we know, of course, that our faith is (or should be) in God, and *that* means everything. It means everything because of who He is.

I have a friend who is a missionary to the lost in Kansas City and has a real love for the homeless there. One day, she stopped her car to offer a cold drink to a homeless man who was blind in one eye. She asked him whether she could pray for him, and if he had any particular requests. "See this eye," he said, pointing to his blind one, "I want to see out of it." My friend was taken aback a little by his boldness and said, "Ah, I see you are a man of faith!" "Young lady," he replied, "what is the one thing God cannot do?" She thought for a moment, not knowing exactly where he was going with this. *"God cannot fail,"* he said.

He's right. That is why we can have faith, and hope, and confidence in God when we need to step out in bravery. He cannot fail, and He will not fail *us*, either. It is *our Father* we stand upon and gird ourselves up with when we are about to take on whatever we're afraid of. And one of the most beautiful things about Him is that He will use and multiply whatever faith we have at that given moment.

Sometimes our faith is big and strong, like a powerful muscle we can flex, a well-trained weapon that can crush our fears. Other times it may be a small, weakened, fragile faith, seemingly held hostage by the fear itself. But even so, hidden within that faith— like the mustard seed—is power and potential exponentially bigger and greater than it appears, powerful enough to overcome the fear, *if activated*. Again, that's where your grafted-in heart comes in, because it's all about remembering who we are, whom we belong to, and who God is. When you think about some of the bravest biblical heroes—Joshua, David, Moses, even Gideon—their deep knowledge of those three things are what they each had in common and what ultimately made them the great men they were. Or how about Rahab, Ruth, or Esther? Their courage also made them legendary. But none of these great heroes had confidence in themselves based on their circumstances or their abilities; each was able to do brave things because of the faith they possessed, the faith that was rightly placed in God and in their relationship with Him. And though we can and should look up to them and follow their examples, being brave doesn't have to look like marching into battle, foiling plots, or leading a revolution.

Sometimes brave doesn't look like you think it does. Sometimes being brave looks like the moment when you're sitting on your bedroom floor drenched in your own tears, that you sit up, wipe your face, and choose hope in some small way. Sometimes brave looks like confessing to someone else that you need help. Brave can be cranking up your worship music and forcing yourself to sing along when you feel like you hate yourself and everyone around you. Brave is choosing to do that one thing you don't want to do because Jesus is whispering that it's the right thing to do; it's listening to and obeying that whisper when everything in you is screaming lies, condemnation, and destruction. Brave is not giving up when it gets hard or messy. Brave is a choice. *It's a faith-based choice to be that overcomer we are absolutely destined to be.* And do you know what Jesus promises us in return for being brave?

> He who overcomes, I will make him a pillar in the temple of My God, and he will not go out from it anymore; and I will write on him the name of My God, and the name

of the city of My God, the new Jerusalem, which comes down out of heaven from My God, and My new name. … He who overcomes, *I will grant to him to sit down with Me on My throne,* as I also overcame and sat down with My Father on His throne.

—Revelation 3:12, 21 NASB

REAL COURAGE IS VULNERABLE; VULNERABILITY TAKES COURAGE

Do you remember at the beginning of the chapter I said that we need to stop avoiding our issues because they might be uncomfortable and messy to face? Vulnerability is uncomfortable and messy … at least at first, if you're new to it. It's kind of like removing some of your protective armor—not the armor of God, but the armor we construct to protect ourselves from getting hurt. Vulnerability doesn't mean sharing your darkest secrets indiscriminately, but it does mean choosing to lay bare a part of yourself that you might instinctively want to protect. It's a willingness to display weakness, softness, tenderness, and openness. It's like surrendering a piece of yourself to another. It's being able to admit that you have shortcomings, that you don't have all the answers, that sometimes you are afraid. The real irony is that it actually requires courage to allow yourself to be vulnerable. The more protected you are, the safer you feel, the less danger there is to face. When you remove some of that protection and then head into risky territory—that takes courage! And if you remember that courage comes from the heart, and vulnerability is essentially removing some of the protective shield from your heart, you can see that both courage and vulnerability come from the very same place.

Vulnerability is what allows true courage to be able to come forth. It also allows us to not only be honest with ourselves but also relatable to others. It's what makes us *human*. More than that, it actually makes us like *Jesus*! In many ways, and in the best ways, Jesus was the perfect example of what it means to be both brave and vulnerable at the same time:

- He came to us vulnerable, as a newborn baby, born to young parents who were not yet married when He was conceived—vulnerable to scorn and disgrace. He was born poor, among animals in a small stable, and before He was even two years old, His family had to flee to Egypt to protect His life.

- He chose to lay aside His divinity and power and live as a man—a simple carpenter.

- His heart was often moved with compassion and He allowed others to see it. He laughed and wept openly.

- He allowed himself to touch—even embrace—the ritually unclean, the sick, and the dead.

- He shared deep friendship with the lowly, the outcasts, and the disreputable.

- He was afraid and distressed in the garden of Gethsemane and wanted His closest friends with Him.

- He suffered tremendous physical, emotional, and spiritual agony on the cross.

YET

- He faced people who mocked Him every day.

- He faced people who were conspiring to kill Him every day.

- He encountered numerous demons and Satan himself, face-to-face.

- He always spoke the truth and He never swayed from His mission.

- He knew when and how His life would end, yet He did not turn away from the task He came for.

Obviously, this is an abbreviated list, but it illustrates the point that Jesus lived His life with His heart wide open, despite the risks He faced. He knew who He was, whom He belonged to, and who God was. Jesus told us that we should come to the kingdom and to the Father "as little children"—little children who are, by nature, vulnerable and open, humble and dependent. Paul even pleaded with believers in Corinth to remain open and vulnerable in relationship to him and those ministering with him:

> We have spoken freely to you, Corinthians; our heart has been opened wide to you. Our affection for you is not restricted, but you are restricted in your affections for us. Now as a fair exchange—I speak as to my children—open wide your hearts to us also.
>
> —2 Corinthians 6:11–13 NET

During the earlier days of my healing process, I came across an online seminar by Brené Brown called "The Power of Vulnerability," which is an eight-hour course based on her wildly popular TED Talk. If you haven't already heard of her, Brené Brown is a research sociologist at the University of Houston who has spent the past thirteen years studying vulnerability, shame, courage, and worthiness. A number of years ago, she was conducting a research study on our need for connection, and stumbled upon a surprising correlation. She found that, in interviewing people about their experiences with connection, they ended up telling her more stories about their experiences with *disconnection*. She said,

> "So very quickly—really about six weeks into this research—I ran into this unnamed thing that absolutely unraveled connection in a way that I didn't understand or had never seen. And so I pulled back out of the research and thought, *I need to figure out what this is.* And it turned out to be shame. And shame is really easily understood as the fear of disconnection: Is there something about me that, if other people know it or see it, that I won't be worthy of connection? … What underpinned this shame, this 'I'm not good enough,'—which, we all know that feeling: 'I'm not _____ enough. I'm not thin enough, rich enough, beautiful enough, smart enough, promoted enough.' The thing that underpinned this was excruciating vulnerability. This idea of, in order for connection to happen, we have to allow ourselves to be seen, really seen."[2]

As I listened to her talk, I was stunned to see that her research had shown what I had surmised about Adam and Eve in the garden; that shame was a direct result of being "disconnected." As she delved further into her research, Brown discovered that one variable separated people who had a strong sense of love and belonging from those who struggled to find it: their sense of worthiness. That led her to study those people who felt worthy of the love and belonging they received, people she refers to as "whole-hearted." What did those people have in common? Two strong traits emerged: 1) courage and 2) vulnerability.

> "They believed that what made them vulnerable made them beautiful. They didn't talk about vulnerability being comfortable, nor did they really talk about it being excruciating—as I had heard it earlier in the shame interviewing. They just talked about it being necessary. They talked about the willingness to say, 'I love you' first … the willingness to do something where there are no guarantees … the willingness to breathe through waiting for the doctor to call after your mammogram. They're willing to invest in a relationship that may or may not work out. They thought this was fundamental."[3]

So if shame comes from a "fear of disconnection," and courage and vulnerability lead to "whole-heartedness," then it would stand to reason that *courage and vulnerability are the antidotes to shame* … the cure for shame in the orphan heart!

THE HERO'S JOURNEY IS OUR JOURNEY

Finally, I want to talk about another surprising connection I have come across in my own grafting-in process, and that is the connection between our journey and something called "The Hero's Journey." I learned about The Hero's Journey from my eldest son, Erik, who came back recently from studying filmmaking in Australia. Erik explained to me that The Hero's Journey is the basic plot template or structure of nearly every movie or story you can think of. Joseph Campbell first introduced the concept in 1949 in his book on comparative mythology, *The Hero with a Thousand Faces,* and it outlines twelve steps in the journey (for an excellent two-minute visual summary, watch Iskander Krayenbosch's animated creation at: https://vimeo.com/140767141).[4] My summary of those twelve steps for you, based on this brilliant video, is as follows:

1. The story begins with an average person in an ordinary world ...

2. When suddenly, s/he is called to adventure!

3. The average person initially refuses the call and tries to run away from his/her destiny.

4. During that time, s/he meets a mentor who ultimately helps him/her ...

5. "Cross the threshold" into accepting the call to adventure.

6. The "emerging hero" faces tests and trials, wins friends and encounters enemies.

7. S/he must face some of her/his worst fears in the "innermost cave."

8. A great battle takes place; s/he must overcome evil and

her/his supreme enemy, and this will change his/her life forever.

9. Having won the battle, the hero receives a great reward.

10. The hero journeys the "road back home."

11. But not before his/her "resurrection" into a new person.

12. The hero returns back home, but "things will never be the same again."

You and I are heroes on a journey. The Bible is an ongoing narrative, a story on a timeline that begins when God created the world and continues on through history, to this very day and beyond, into eternity. You and I are part of that greater story and we each have stories of our own with plots that are unfolding as we live our lives day by day. I'm not quite sure that we only have one "hero's journey" in our lifetime; I suspect some of us have many of these journeys to make. The journey to lead our orphan heart home to the Father is one of those most critical journeys— ultimately, we will be resurrected into new people, and things will never be the same again if we find our way back home. But we need to accept the call.

Finally, if you think about all the great movies and tales and all the great heroes, there is always something really special about the hero that draws us to him or her. That special something is *vulnerability amidst their great courage.* We love to watch them discover who they are and the courage they didn't know they had until they had to activate it. And inevitably, the "resurrected self" they bring back home has a new softness, a new love for others, a new perspective; and because of this, their lives truly cannot ever be the same. So it will be with us if we keep on the journey. We have the greatest Mentor anyone could ever have, showing us the ropes and equipping us for the battles. We can do this. We can be heroes. We can be brave.

Connection

Reach out to me, O Lord.
Reach out and touch the face of the one who seeks you,
the one who longs for you,
the one whose very breath depends upon your grace.
For I look to you;
my eyes are fixed upon you and I have postured my heart towards you,
yet I cannot fully live without your embrace.

A touch from your majestic Fatherly hand brings hope,
healing,
peace,
life.
It releases the floodgates of your steadfast, loyal love into my parched soul
and it changes me.

Lord, you have my heart, my devotion, my whole life—
I give all of myself to you as an offering, meager as it is.
Burn away the chaff of my life and harvest the wheat;
make me like you, O Bread of life, and be pleased with me.
Father me, teach me, love me as only You can.
I reach for you and I know you are near, yet I wait for your touch.
Here I am, Lord.

CHAPTER 10

It's All About Relationship

The spiritual life is a gift. It is a gift of the Holy Spirit, who lifts us up into the kingdom of God's love. But to say that being lifted up into the kingdom of love is a divine gift does not mean that we wait passively until the gift is offered to us.

—Henri J. M. Nouwen[1]

Hopefully by now you are beginning to take some steps along your journey or are at least mapping out the route you will take. In this chapter, we are going to look at some practical ways to begin cultivating and nurturing a much closer Father-daughter or Father-son relationship than you have been able to experience before. At this point (if you've already started down the road), you will have identified and defeated some major lies, begun yielding and surrendering your control, your fears—even your will—to the Father's will, and letting His love "surround your surrender." You will have identified some of the people or things that have taken the Father's place in your heart and cleared them out, making room for Him. And you will have chosen to take all of this on with courage and vulnerability, even if it gets difficult and messy and takes longer than you hoped it would. Take a moment now and thank the Lord for His goodness toward you, for His steadfast love, and for His help in all you are endeavoring to do.

An Important Distinction

Before we get into the practicalities, I want to make an important distinction here. I've received well-meaning advice over the years I've been seeking to truly understand God as Father that I shouldn't be striving for it—that I should "just rest, and it'll come." I tried that, honestly and earnestly. It didn't work in my case. Not that it wasn't worth a try, and maybe coming from your own unique situation, it would be important to evaluate whether you are striving when you should be just receiving. I completely agree with the message I was given, which was that we don't ever have to strive for the Father's love—He gives it freely and abundantly. The distinction I want to make is between striving and *doing the work it takes to have a real relationship*, one that is whole and healthy and growing.

Here's one way to look at it: Think about going to the doctor to get your eyes checked; you're sitting in the chair and looking through that big contraption at the chart on the wall. The doctor starts out with everything looking relatively clear, then she flips a new lens over the original lens ("Is this better, or worse?") to see if it makes a difference. It's kind of like that with us. Our hurts, sins, traumas, bitterness, and so on are the blurry lenses that get layered over the clear ones, distorting what we are able to see. Until we remove those lenses, it won't matter what we're trying to look at; everything we see will be distorted and corrupted because we're looking at it through the wrong lens.

We don't need to strive for the Father's love, but we won't see it, feel it, or experience it as it really is until we are able to remove the distorted lenses we're looking through. That is one part of the work we need to do, and the steps I've outlined earlier should help in that regard. Then there is the day-to-day kind of work that good relationships require. I do not have to strive for or earn my husband's love, for instance. I know I have it and that I will not lose it. The same is true for him. However, there is always work to be done to keep our marriage strong, our love active and growing, and our relationship healthy. It's the same thing with God, except that God always has His act together, so it's really just you and I that need to work at it on our ends! Some things we need to do are so basic and almost ordinary, we don't do them because we forget how important they actually are. Giving the Lord our time and attention, set aside just for Him, is a big one.

Devotional Time

This subject brought up quite a bit of angst in me for many years. As a young mother of three, I would wake up each morning feeling like my feet hit the ground running as I stepped out of bed. My days were always full and active, taking care of my children full time, trying to earn some money part time through various job opportunities, nurturing friendships, and serving the Lord through several different ministries. Many nights my husband and I barely had the energy to high-five one another before we collapsed back in bed. I would feel immensely guilty when I heard other people (especially other young mothers) talk about their "quiet time" with the Lord. The only quiet time I was having was when my eyelids were shut!

And it wasn't just a time thing; I had plenty of issues going on that made me feel like it was all I could possibly do just to get through the day with everyone intact, myself included. God had so much grace for me in those days. I believe He understood I was doing all I was equipped to do at that point. I look back now and see how good He was to me, how much He loved me to meet me where I was, and to meet me even more so when I was able to turn my full attention to Him. He does give us grace in those times and does not withhold Himself from us—but I know we cannot possibly be entering in to all that is available to us during those times either. As my children grew and my life and schedule went through significant changes, I found it easy to justify the same patterns (or lack thereof) of spending time with the Lord. We were always busy, there was always some crisis arising, always something that seemed to take precedent. It was so easy to feel and declare that we simply could not afford to sit down and take time out to be with God.

Yet as time ticked by and the demands on me as a mother shifted, my own aching emptiness began to rise to the surface. As I continued to shove it back down and try to keep busy, other things began to pop up, too—loneliness that couldn't be alleviated, fear, restlessness … you see where this is going. The Holy Spirit was beginning to prod at me that it was time to take care of these things. And "taking care of these things" required *time*. Our time is another thing we need to give to the Lord as a sacrificial offering. It helps me to think of it that way, anyway. Some of my time had to be devoted to seeking prayer ministry and counseling to address the issues that grew out of my orphan heart.

Most significant for me, however, was conceding some of my time to be spent in prayer and devotional study. I said earlier that if you really want change, you have to be willing to make changes. I had to say that to myself first and repeat it often. For me, it was doing the unthinkable—waking up (that is, getting up) earlier than my schedule required to spend time with God. I have never been a morning person, and by that I mean I *hated mornings*! My first waking thought every morning was usually, *When can I get back to sleep?* But by this time, I was so desperate to know the Father. With everything I had experienced—all the loss and heartache—I knew I could not go on living anymore without knowing what it meant to be a daughter and experiencing my Father's love.

God wants our time and attention because He loves us and wants to be with us. How can we honestly expect real relationship to happen without giving Him our undivided time and attention? We wouldn't expect a deep, loving, reciprocal relationship with our earthly fathers if we never called them or spent time with them except for when we needed something. A good parent loves to provide for his or her children, but no parent wants to feel that is all they are good for. Recently I read of this encounter that Pastor John Arnott had with the Lord during one of his prayer times:

> While reading in Exodus, I related to the deep and searching prayer of Moses, "Show me your glory" (33:18). I immediately cried out, "O Lord, why are You so hard to find? Why is it so difficult to be close to You?" I was thinking in terms of His holiness and my unholiness. But He spoke to me in my heart, and His answer was one of the most precious things I ever heard God say to me: "When

I reveal my heart to someone, I become very vulnerable." I had never thought of God as being vulnerable. I thought of Him as omniscient, omnipotent and omnipresent, which, of course, He is. But He was sharing with me His own desire for fellowship, relationship and intimacy— and I was surprised. That's the nature of love—it needs to be freely and willingly reciprocated. He drew near to have fellowship and intimacy with me, and I was deeply hurting Him by immediately asking for things. … We are often oblivious to the fact that God wants an intimate relationship with us. Intimacy cannot be a one-sided love affair. It flows out of humble, vulnerable hearts.[2]

It is just about unimaginable that the Creator of the Universe wants alone time with us—but it's true! And I don't think He cares very much that it looks a certain way or that you read a certain thing or pray a certain way. He will bless you wherever you begin, even if it all feels awkward and perfunctory at first. You can pick a daily Bible reading plan or follow a study, or begin with a devotional book. Or, you could try what I have tried: a combination of things. When I begin my quiet time, I usually have a couple of daily devotional books by different authors, my Bible, my journal, and at least one biblical book in which I read one chapter a day. For me, this helps my focus to have a few short readings to do first (while the coffee takes effect) and one longer one that explores a topic in greater depth than the devotionals. Given the fact that I use books by different authors, it's pretty amazing that almost every day, the message I receive from the Lord is consistent and clearly laid out in each book, including the corresponding Bible verses.

I also have been learning so much from reading pieces written by believers of different historical time periods: contemporary, classical, and ancient. There is so much wisdom to be gained, so many beautiful perspectives to appreciate and apprehend, it would be a disservice to limit yourself to reading only those works by current pastors and theologians. I cannot adequately express the depth and importance of these morning devotional times I've been having with the Lord. It's made a convert out of me—I don't know if I'd say I am a morning person now, but I do look forward to and love the mornings in a way I never had before. Early mornings work for me in that they are the only times I know I won't be interrupted. It doesn't matter what time of day yours ultimately is, as long as it's your time alone with God, uninterrupted and set aside just for you and Him.

JOURNALING

Ah, journaling … the thing that has brought up almost as much angst in me as devotional time. You see, I'm not suggesting for you to do anything I haven't first resisted myself! If you are already having a regular quiet time and keeping a journal, you are in a great position (but keep reading on!). Those of you who don't, I'm here to encourage you to do this, too. The idea of journaling was a serious stretch for someone like me, who barely had it in them to keep up a calendar. But again and again, the annoying suggestion kept coming up with people trying to help me along my path. I just couldn't see why it would be helpful to get my thoughts down on paper. There were already more thoughts than I could handle going on inside my head, and the notion that any of them might be there in print … that seemed too much to bear. What if someone read it and thought it was stupid? What if I read it and thought *I* was stupid? I had enough fear and shame rattling around inside me; the last thing I wanted was for something else (especially something this concrete) to stir it up and make it available to the naked eye. No thanks.

Yet this, too, hung around and nagged at me like an irritating little poke every so often. Then one day a friend showed me some poetic phrases and thoughts she had jotted down in her journal, musings on the beauty of the Lord and stuff like that. I thought maybe I could do something like that, plus I told myself I could always use it for sermon notes. So that's where I started: sermon notes and a few flowery love poems to God. Before long, though, those flowery poems evolved into psalms of thanksgiving and longings of my heart. Prayers began to flow, then prophetic words—for myself, for others, for my church. When life turned ugly, my pain and desperation poured out into my journal, alternating between cries for help and declarations of hope. More poems came, and these took on more depth and maturity. Many of them I have included in this book before each chapter.

Let me explain why I chose to include them, and it's not because I think they're great. I don't actually understand poetry well enough to recognize what makes a poem great or not, but I included them for a couple of reasons. One, because they are concrete examples of what I am talking about here, with the added bonus of actually demonstrating courage and vulnerability in allowing what I've written in my private journal to be seen publicly. Second, nearly all of these poems were written a year or so before I began writing this book; as I said, they were expressions of longing and hope that came out of an intensely painful time in my life. I had no idea they would essentially pair up with steps in my own healing, much less with chapters in a book I intended to publish!

I'm sure none of this surprised the Lord, and I'm certain He knew exactly how He would use them.

My point is, journaling for the believer is about more than pouring your guts out on paper; there is an honesty and vulnerability about bringing those thoughts out of our heads and into the light. We can see them for what they are—for the good, the bad, and the ugly. The bad stuff loses its power and its bite once it's out of our heads, and the good … well, it kind of takes root and gives us a place to stand upon to push through to the next level. And if we submit what we write and our whole journaling process to the Lord, we can be sure that He will use it for our good and for His glory. Our old journals can hold testimonies of answered prayers, memories of dreams and promises, and ideas that could become fodder for something new and creative right now.

It's been in my journal that I have taken my first baby steps in trying to talk to God like He really is my father and I really am His daughter. Writing it out was a concrete way to practice functioning in that role. I was desperate, and my desperation helped me to push past long-held fears, inhibitions, and shame-based avoidance to try new avenues to go after what I really wanted. He did not disappoint me, and He won't disappoint you, either.

> But when they in their trouble turned to the Lord, the God of Israel, and [in desperation, earnestly] sought Him, He was found by them.
>
> —2 Chronicles 15:4 AMPC

"Tell Me Again About the Night I Was Born"

The above title is the name of a children's book written by Jamie Lee Curtis that came out just before we adopted our first daughter, Noel. We were not only preparing for our first baby girl, we were also preparing for our first adoption, and learning all we could about how to be good adoptive parents to her. One of the first things I learned was the importance of her story, and the importance of telling it. I think all (or certainly, most) children love to hear the story of how they came into this world, and I think the preciousness of the subject deserves a story worth the telling. This is especially true for children who have been adopted. For one, their birth itself was probably not as celebrated or embraced as it usually is for a majority of children raised within their birth families. There are often gaps between their birth and their adoption; some, like two of ours, have years in between—years filled with unhappiness, fear, and pain, certainly not celebration. Adopted children need to know not only their birth stories and their lives before adoption, they also need to hear all the details that tell them they are valuable, they were worth waiting for, and that they are loved:

> Tell me again about the night I was born. Tell me again how you would adopt me and be my parents ... tell me again about the first time you held me in your arms ...[3]

Hearing their adoption story is necessary for the adoptee's healing and bonding, and for assimilating into the family. Often, when they are little, adopted children want to hear their story every night before bed; even when they're older and would cringe at that suggestion, they still need to hear their story regularly even if they don't ask for it—for the same reasons. Not long ago, the Lord asked me something surprising. He wanted me to ask Him to tell me my story as He saw it, and before I could even get out all the words, a slideshow of memories started to play through my mind. But the strangest thing was, I saw them, not as myself, remembering events, but through the Father's eyes.

I saw myself opening gifts on Christmas when I was five or six, and I could *feel* the intense love and joy and pride of the Father watching me. I saw myself learning to ride a bike, going to my first overnight camp, walking across the stage at my high school graduation. For the first time in my life, I felt—almost *remembered*—the Father was there with me—watching, loving, protecting—through all those events. It was so overwhelming I had to ask Him to stop! And since that time, He has reminded me to ask Him again, "Father ... *Papa* ... tell me my story." If I can quiet myself down and push away distractions, He tells me. He shows me.

This might be a weird one for you, and a bizarre, even embarrassing suggestion for me to make. I get it. But if you are anything at all like me, you have spent years living from a place of rejection and abandonment and the last thing you feel is that you are worth celebrating—or worth an idyllic bedtime story of your own. Maybe you would do anything to have heard your story told by your mom or dad when you were little, or maybe you long for it still, now that you are grown.

Part of hearing your adoption story is not just hearing *that* you are loved, but *why* you are loved, and *how* He loves you. I know that the Father loves to answer those questions—He longs to answer them—but you must ask the questions. Like other adopted children, it is essential that you hear your story; that you see, and understand, and begin to learn it by heart. Your story tells you who you are, where you have come from, why you are here. Like in the Hero's Journey we learned about in the previous chapter, you need to discover the part you are meant to play in your story, and how the events in your life all fit in the framework. Part of our struggle as orphans is that, as John Eldridge puts it, "we have lost our story." In his book *EPIC: The Story God Is Telling*, Eldridge encourages us to recognize our story within the larger story—that is, the ongoing narrative of God's people in the Bible:

> We find ourselves in the middle of a story that is sometimes wonderful, sometimes awful, often a confusing mixture of both, and we haven't a clue how to make sense of it all. It's like we're holding in our hands some pages torn out of a book. These pages are the days of our lives. Fragments of a story. They seem important, or at least we long to know they are, but what does it all mean? If only we could find the book that contains the rest of the story.[4]

The problem is, we often don't even know and understand the torn-out pages we're holding, the ones that tell us our own story. Worse, what we do know is usually badly translated, distorted by our own pain and what we believe about ourselves that has been informed by other people or even the devil himself. This is why it is so important to ask the *Father* to tell us our story—not only what has happened thus far in our lives but also to help us write the empty chapters that remain. Sons and daughters begin to know and understand who they are when they hear their own story firsthand, told by a loving parent who is just as eager to tell it to them.

Father ... Papa ... tell me again about the night I was born. Tell me again how happy You were to adopt me and make me Your own. Tell me again about the first time You saw me and held me in Your arms ...

FILTERING WHAT GOES IN

My husband and I started dating right before college, and fortunately for both of us we attended the same one. It was a large campus with many thousands of students, but that didn't really matter—we were in our own little world. Yes, we had friends. We socialized, went to class, got involved in a few activities, but mostly we were just "us," him and me, in our own little world. There is something naturally isolating about falling in love and deepening a relationship—whether it's a new romance, a new baby, or like us in more recent years, a newly expanded family. You need that time at first to devote to each other, to really get to know one another, to bond, to figure out how to make the relationship work, to develop your own special language. Sure, you still have friends and family that you maintain relationship with, you still have your jobs and responsibilities, church, "real life." But for a while, everything else just kind of gets back-burnered, bumped down on the list of priorities. You don't have as much time or energy or even the desire to keep up with the news, and a lot of time you end up educating yourself more about the life situation you're in. You might be reading magazines about weddings or marriage, books about child development, and blogs about breastfeeding, tantrums, sibling rivalry, or even attachment disorder. You're in your own world, and for a time that isolation is necessary.

About six months or so into my journey of coming to really know God as Father, the Lord told me that I should become hidden in Him for a season. I have to say that I understood exactly what He meant right away, and I was relieved. I had been walking through many months of tackling those "Four *S*'s" (as described in chapter 7) and I felt exhausted, vulnerable, and raw from the process. Hiding myself in Him was an invitation to find refuge and protection, rest and nurturing, in the safety of His covering:

> The Lord is my light and my salvation—Whom shall I
>   fear?
> The Lord is the refuge and fortress of my life—Whom
>   shall I dread?
> When the wicked came against me to eat up my flesh,
> my adversaries and my enemies, they stumbled and fell.
> Though an army encamp against me, my heart will not
>   fear;
> Though war arise against me, even in this I am confident.
> One thing I have asked of the Lord, and that I will seek:
> That I may dwell in the house of the Lord [in His
>   presence] all the days of my life,
> to gaze upon the beauty [the delightful loveliness and
>   majestic grandeur] of the Lord
> and to meditate in His temple.
> For in the day of trouble He will hide me in His shelter;
> in the secret place of His tent He will hide me; He will
>   lift me up on a rock.
> And now my head will be lifted up above my enemies
>   around me,
> in His tent I will offer sacrifices with shouts of joy;
> I will sing, yes, I will sing praises to the Lord.
> Hear, O Lord, when I cry aloud;
> be gracious and compassionate to me and answer me.

When You said, "Seek My face [in prayer, require My
presence as your greatest need],"
my heart said to You, "Your face, O Lord, I will seek [on
the authority of Your word]."
Do not hide Your face from me, do not turn Your servant
away in anger;
You have been my help; do not abandon me nor leave
me, O God of my salvation!
Although my father and my mother have abandoned
me,
Yet the Lord will take me up [adopt me as His child].
Teach me Your way, O Lord, and lead me on a level path
because of my enemies [who lie in wait].
Do not give me up to the will of my adversaries, for false
witnesses have come against me;
they breathe out violence.
I would have despaired had I not believed that I would
see the goodness of the Lord
in the land of the living.
Wait for and confidently expect the Lord;
Be strong and let your heart take courage;
Yes, wait for and confidently expect the Lord.

—Psalm 27 AMPC

I lived and breathed this psalm (and others) during this
time. As I often meditated on the phrase *hidden in Him*, I began
to picture what that might look like and what it might feel like. I
think it was the first time I was able to imagine myself sitting on
the Father's lap, concealed in the folds of His magnificent sleeves.
Sometimes I felt He wanted me to just sit there quietly and feel

safe, to rest, even fall asleep there. Other times, I felt it was there that He wanted to teach me about being His daughter.

What was clear very quickly was that I was going to have to isolate and filter very carefully what I allowed in my spirit, my mind, and my heart. Much of the work I did prior to that time involved getting things out that didn't belong there; now it was time to carefully monitor and protect what was going in. The details may look different for you, but for me they involved staying off all social media and limiting my Internet usage in general, choosing carefully whom I spent time with—limiting phone calls and sometimes even limiting the topics of conversation to the ones I discerned would be "safe" and life-giving to me at that time. In addition to the quiet time I spent with the Lord, I became an avid reader of great spiritual books, drinking in all I could hold on the topics of forgiveness, healing, the goodness of God, God as Father, how to walk through times of suffering, and so on. I read so many wonderful, precious, life-giving books that I have no doubt the Lord directed me to personally. I wasn't stockpiling knowledge, though—I was retraining my mind, renewing it, pouring a healing salve into my very wounded heart.

One morning, I attended a church where the worship leader sang a song he wrote called "Home." Because I didn't know it, I couldn't sing along, and therefore just closed my eyes and let the words fill my spirit, as I had been doing with all my reading. As he sang, I felt my head against the Father's chest and realized I was swaying as He danced with me:

> You called my name louder than the crowd; You have
> captured my attention
> You brought me here, and I don't need to run; You will
> let me stay forever

It's where I belong, it's where I am found—in Your love

It's where I'm made whole, I'm given a home—in Your love

Now I can breathe; and I don't need to strive, I have finally found a family

And I believe You won't let me fall; You are ever faithful towards me

It's where I belong, it's where I am found—in Your love

It's where I'm made whole, I'm given a home—in Your love

I am home, now I see heart restored

I believe Father's love covers me;

no more fear—I am free.

—"Home," CityWorship, *I Am Home*[5]

There are people who have experiences like this all the time, but this was an absolute first for me—a life-changing moment I will never forget. I danced with the Father. The things I had prayed for all my life were happening at last! I bought the album, and once I was back home, I played that song often to remind myself of that incredible experience, and then I had an idea.

Do you remember making (or having someone else make you) a "mix tape" of special songs that reminded you of something significant—like summer vacation songs you listened to with your best friend, or the songs you heard when you were dating and madly in love? I had the idea to make myself a playlist of songs that reminded me of significant encounters with God, "love songs" from the Father to me, or from me to Him. I know that sounds corny, but I did it, and I played them often, even as I was going to sleep at night. I wanted to get those songs down in my heart where they would stay. I kept thinking of Zephaniah 3:17, which says, "He will rejoice over you with gladness; he will quiet you by his love; he will exult over you with loud singing." So now I have a collection of the Father's love songs for me, and I know that no one else has that particular playlist … and I am realizing that my whole way of thinking has been changing. I am beginning to see myself through His eyes now, as a daughter who is uniquely loved by her Father. This is new and revolutionary, like nothing else I've ever experienced. And it is wonderful.

I've shared some pretty personal stuff with you in this last section, but I've done so with a purpose. Sometimes it'll take some out-of-the-box thinking and pushing yourself way past your comfort zone to explore uncharted territory. It's vulnerable and courageous and risky for me, putting stuff like this out there and suggesting for you to try it yourself. The details may look different for you—they probably should, at least somewhat. But I want to broaden your thinking about what it may take to pursue the relationship with the Father that you have always wanted. People do all types of silly stuff when they're in love, don't they? This is no different, except the stakes are higher. This is a relationship that will last through all of eternity, and He is worth every bit of the pursuit.

My Father's Eyes

You bid me, "Come! Come into My presence, sit before me."
You invite me in.
Oh, to be invited, to belong, to be welcomed!
I hesitate to rush in, but my heart is already there.
I lean in to clasp the hands of the One who loves me.
He knows me; He has chosen me and has given me a new name.
He is pleased to make me His own.
His hands, they are strong but gentle, and they lead me;
they lead me into His heart.
Into Your heart, Lord, into Your gaze still further I am drawn.
Your eyes, they search me, they know me.
Their righteous love flushes out my shame—no sin or sorrow can hide from them.
I want you to know me, yet I am frightened by what you might find.
Yet search me, Lord, until You find the real me:
crouching, uncertain, naked, raw.
Oh, you who I so hesitantly call Father—your eyes, they frighten me;
yet to you I run for comfort.
Down and down they search until they reach bottom—and a smile breaks forth
as they pronounce me, "clean and acceptable."
Yet not only that, but "worthy to be loved."
I cannot fathom my own depths, but you have done it and have loved me still.
And your eyes remain true and pure, even having seen it all.
Is it possible I am loved this thoroughly, this completely?

You say, "Yes! And even more so, yes!"
My heart cracks and breaks under the weight of this truth.
The cracking and breaking—it is painful to be sure,
but such is the process of ever-expanding, ever-opening wider, and wider still.
Because a little girl's heart cannot contain her Father's great love.
It must grow bigger.
It must grow stronger.
It must grow wiser.
It must expand to house the truth of Your love and make a home for it there.
And though it might feel lost in the bottomless chasm,
the little girl's heart has found a home—
a home in her Father's eyes.

CHAPTER 11

Arriving Home

"I have come home at last! This is my real country! I belong here. This is the land I have been looking for all my life, though I never knew it till now. … Come further up, come further in!"

—C. S. Lewis, *The Last Battle*[1]

The above quote comes from what is probably my favorite passage in all of literature—the last scene of *The Last Battle*, the culmination of the whole series of the CHRONICLES OF NARNIA, where the children finally arrive "home." I have read that book at least a dozen times, and I still can't get through it without crying because my spirit so longs to arrive there, too. And though you and I have not yet reached our ultimate destination, I know I can finally say for myself that I have indeed reached my home, at least the one this side of heaven. I pray you will, too.

OUR CHOICE TO CHOOSE

As an adoptive parent for the past twenty years, I have learned much about orphans—their struggles with identity and their pasts, their strong spirits to survive and thrive despite their circumstances, and how the rejection, abandonment, and separation from their natural parents leaves a devastating wake in their lives. The miracle of adopting children isn't that we pull them out of their orphaned state, providing a safe place and all the material things they need; it's the complete shift in status and identity that we offer: of belonging, of value, of love, and of sonship. The legal transaction of adoption makes this offer a covenant, but it cannot cause the orphan to internalize that outer reality. That has to be their choice. The real miracle of adoption happens when they choose you back; when they choose to recognize their place with you and all that it means, when they choose to accept and receive and belong to you in return.

We have a Father who has rescued us out of our orphaned state. He gives us a safe place and promises to provide us with everything we need. He gives us a new name, a new identity, and we belong to Him. He calls us sons and daughters, His treasured possessions. He loves us with an unfailing, steadfast love, and He has adopted us. The question now is: Will you choose Him back? Will you choose to recognize your place in Him and all that it means, and choose to accept and receive and belong to Him in return?

OUR CHOICE TO TRUST

The choice to trust, at this point, should not only be an act of our will, but the chosen posture of our heart. As we make the choice to fully embrace our adoption, we also need to permanently part ways with our orphan heart and choose to fully embrace the new heart we are given: the heart of a son or daughter. And this heart trusts God … in all things. Easy to say, hard to do—I know. But let's take the first half of that—it *is* easy to say it. We can begin there, speaking like a son or daughter who trusts the Father. We can speak out that trust to others; we can speak it to ourselves.

When I wrote the poem that precedes this chapter, it was during the beginning stages of teaching my heart to assume the posture of trust. It takes incredible vulnerability, and therefore trust, to lock eyes with the Father, knowing there is nothing you can possibly hide in His presence. The exposure, the emotional nakedness of that experience would make anyone want to bolt right out of there and draw inward … yet His love and His kindness are so compelling it is impossible to leave. And so you sit there, letting His eyes search you, see you, know you, and love you. You are there in His presence with His hands tenderly holding yours, and you are safe. There is nothing—*nothing*—that can snatch you out of His hands. Not sickness, not death, not anything you can think of. Picture yourself sitting there in front of Him, locking eyes, holding hands. What can you say to argue against His outrageous love for you?

"Lord, I am unworthy!"

Yes, but you are worth everything to me.

"Lord, I've done terrible things!"

Yes, but I have made you clean.

"Father … I'm afraid."

I know you are. But I am here and you are safe, and I am not leaving.

The sheer weight of this truth is almost too much to bear, and those truths cannot find a home within the orphan heart. That is why the orphan heart needs to be dismantled, torn apart, and broken open. The new heart we're given is bigger, wider, and grander, for it will, in time, hold much more than an orphan heart could ever hold. But it all must begin from a new place of trust.

OUR CHOICE TO LOVE AND BE LOVED

Arriving home with the Father necessitates our choice to love and be loved. First and foremost, it is a choice to lavish our love on Him and to receive His love for us. Some of us may find one or the other of those things to be a stretch, but that is okay for now. We only need now to choose it regardless of how uncomfortable it might make us feel. Choosing to lavish our love on the Father means an actual practice of doing it not only in words but also in deeds. We must dedicate time to being with Him not only in prayers of petition but also in worship, praise, and thanksgiving. Spending time in His Word and quieting ourselves down to reflect on it and listen for His voice is necessary also. It is a discipline. When the feelings of love and affection are there, it is a joy-filled one. But even if we can't yet access the feelings of love toward Him, we must lean on faith that they will eventually come with time and practice.

Remember that both giving love and receiving it are acts of surrender and of sacrificing our control. For me, being able to receive and feel His love have been a challenge; surprisingly, my first reaction when I do begin to sense it is to try to stop it or push it away. It's not that I want to reject it, but it is a conditioned response of self-protection that has become a powerful habit for me. As soon as I am aware of it, I have to choose to resist my resistance—that is, to just let go and surrender to what He's doing. Sometimes I have to almost talk myself through the receiving-love process, telling myself to *receive, believe, feel, and respond.* Giving and receiving love seem like they should be an automatic response—and often they are—but we shouldn't get discouraged if we have to teach ourselves to do it.

Look at it this way: Many new mothers instantly bond to and love their babies immediately after delivery, but not all of them. Some have to go through the motions for a while until the feelings come. In fact, most adoptions are like that. We make the choice to love right off the bat, and there is excitement and infatuation in the early days, but the deep feelings of love usually take some time to develop. Then we, as adoptive parents, tell ourselves, "It's just part of the process." So it is sometimes with "adopting" the Father back.

There is a "part two" of the choice to love and be loved, and that involves others. For most of us, it won't be a radical shift from not loving people or not feeling loved at all by others, but it is more a shift in *how* we give, receive, and even perceive love. This goes back to the lenses I talked about in the previous chapter; we have to check ourselves to see if we are looking through the blurry ones—the lenses corrupted by hurt, bitterness, resentment, and so on—and remind ourselves that we are now looking through the clear lenses of a son or daughter. We should be seeing with the eyes of the Father, and loving with our grafted-in hearts. If we choose to take this step, there is a new depth of love and intimacy within relationships that is available to us because we are secure in the love of our Father.

We can love more freely and fully accept the love others have to give if we are less afraid of their rejection. We can freely receive love from others if we are free from unrealistic expectations that they will meet the needs only God can meet. We can be less afraid if we are confident that, no matter what happens in our relationships here on earth, we can run to our heavenly Father at any point and receive all the love we could ever need. This not only gives us greater potential to love our friends and family better, it also equips us to love others outside our own circles—loving our neighbors as ourselves, as Jesus calls us to do.

That leads us to part three of choosing to love and be loved, which involves loving ourselves. Loving ourselves as sons and daughters is not a self-centered version of self-love; it is something much different. It has more to do with having respect and value for ourselves because we recognize to Whom we belong—if the Father deems us worthy of love, so should we. If the Father has compassion on us when we are hurting or when we fail, so should we. We should look upon ourselves and treat ourselves with kindness. If we have been grafted in, it is no longer appropriate for us to recite self-defeating mantras, allow ourselves to be engulfed in shame, or otherwise treat ourselves more harshly than we would treat a friend. For most of us, the idea of "loving ourselves" is awkward, uncomfortable, and even feels wrong … yet, done within these parameters, it is a hallmark of emotional and spiritual wholeness.

Our Choice to Make Ourselves at Home

When we brought home our two children from Uganda, our youngest son, Martin, could not wait to check out the whole house. He ran from room to room (beginning with his own bedroom, of course), wanting to know where everything was. For days, he proceeded to open every single drawer, cabinet, and closet, carefully inspecting the contents. Every knob in the house was turned; every button was pushed. This was his new home, and he wanted to explore every inch of it. Beloved, this needs to be our attitude when we finally arrive home to our Father! We will have all of eternity to get to explore and know it all—if indeed that is even possible—but we dare not wait until we pass out of this world to begin exploring! Our Father's "house" is His kingdom, and we were taught by Jesus Himself to pray for His kingdom to come here on earth as it is in heaven. Part of our purpose as followers of Jesus and children of God is to help spiritual realities break into the natural realm. How can we recognize what is of the kingdom unless we've spent time getting to know what's in there?

So study His Word, read the teachings of Jesus that begin, *"The kingdom of God is like ..."* Get to know the Beatitudes, which my Bible has sub-headed as, "Precepts of the Kingdom Life." As the world grows increasingly darker, it may seem futile to believe in, much less work toward, the kingdom coming to earth as it is in heaven—but that is the very thing Jesus taught us to pray. He would not lead us to ask for and participate in something that is impossible even with His help! I know oftentimes my heart just cannot hope that we could experience heavenly life here on earth. But He said it, and therefore it is true. It is also true that it is the charge and duty of sons and daughters to bring it forth—*we are the plan of action!*

Our Choice to Embrace Freedom

As I write this section, this is the very choice I have had before me. Embracing my newfound freedom. Of course, I chose it up front—at least I thought I had—but it has become clear to me that it is a choice I will need to keep making until I know I've embraced it fully. It reminds me a little of the story of the Hebrew people as they were led out of Egypt. If you can think back with me (or, better yet, reread their story in Exodus), you'll remember how the Hebrews witnessed miracle upon miracle, from the plagues to the parting of the Red Sea. Then, once their enemies were swallowed up inside that very sea, they became a free people, heading toward the promised land. The problem was, they did not yet know how to be free. So their kind and loving Father set out to teach them just that, and rule number one was: *"Freedom looks like complete dependence on Me."* Say what? Freedom is independence, right?

Wrong.

Their independent selves were wandering the Sinai Desert and could not find food or water, much less figure out where they were going. So God provided water from a rock, manna from heaven, and pillars of cloud and fire to direct them when and where they should go. Were they happy with this arrangement? Not for long. They actually began complaining that life was ultimately better for them in Egypt—in captivity! And thus began the cycle—they complained and rebelled, and the Lord disciplined. They repented and obeyed, and the Lord blessed them. He created rules for them to follow (the Mosaic and Deuteronomic covenants and the Ten Commandments) so that He could teach them how to be a free people. The problem was that the Hebrews had spent four hundred years as slaves—that's generation upon generation of oppression, sin, bad habits, and clouded mind-sets—and they had to unlearn all of it in order to be free.

It was a new game with new rules. But as with Adam and Eve in the garden, when God's rules are given for life and freedom, people just seem hardwired to balk at those rules. If we have spent years with a slave's mind-set, it can be surprisingly uncomfortable to operate in true freedom. Our nature, helped along by Satan, often views the enslavement as the more familiar, comfortable, even "safer" option—but it is a deception. And all it takes sometimes is a painful experience, an unforeseen situation, or simple discomfort to lure us right back into desiring slavery over freedom. That's why we need to choose it and embrace it. Even the rules. What are the rules? *The Precepts of the Kingdom Life*. Read those Beatitudes!

CHOOSING TO ABIDE IN HIM

A while back, I rescued a baby bird. My daughter Emilee found it after school on her walk from the bus stop and brought it home. It was so tiny and helpless; it was roughly the size of a grape. It had some feathers but was still pretty naked, and it clearly was not ready to leave the nest—in fact, we went back to where she found it, and the nest had been ravaged and the other birds were dead. I couldn't find anyone to take it for the first few days, so Em and I did everything we could to help it, and truly it was the grace of God that kept that little baby alive. It was so fragile it was almost terrifying to feed it at first. But after a couple of days, hunger and instinct drove it to cry for help, and it finally began begging for its food, which made feeding it much easier.

Now, I am not advocating the methods I used to care for it, as a wild animal really should be cared for by a trained rehabilitator, but the Lord had a powerful lesson for me in caring for this baby bird. Because I loved this little creature so much, I could not resist holding it, petting it, and loving it. It didn't take long for it to respond positively to my attention. It actually seemed to enjoy being held and even seemed to want it, particularly after being fed.

So I'd let it sit there in my palm, with my fingers cupped around it like a nest, until I could feel its little body relax and watch its drowsy eyes begin to close. Then it would tuck its beak under its wing and go to sleep. One day as I sat watching it sleep, the Lord said, *"This is what it means to abide in me."*

Abiding in Him is an ongoing state of resting at peace in His hands, confident that we are safe and secure, intimately connected to Him. Anywhere we may go, and whatever we may do, those hands will carry us there—if we choose to make it our home. Jesus even said, "No one is able to snatch them out of the Father's hand" (John 10:29).

The Four Chambers of the Grafted-In Heart

New home, new life, new rules, new heart. As beloved sons and daughters, we have received a heart transplant of the best kind: a heart of flesh for a heart of stone. A grafted-in heart for the heart of an orphan. Remember the Four Chambers of the Orphan Heart? Soul Loneliness, Restless Wandering, Shame, and Fear? Well, now … new heart, new chambers!

Exchanged for the Chamber of Soul Loneliness: *Fellowship*

We never have to be lonely again. Not at a heart level, anyway. Now we are given an internal, eternal family that will never leave. All relational persons we could ever need reside within our heart and provide a constant companionship we can rely on and turn to … *always.*

Exchanged for the Chamber of Restless Wandering: *Home*

Home is where we can return to at any given moment … and belong. It's our Father's house, and the doors are open, the lights are on, the fire is lit, and the table is set. We can kick off our shoes and dive onto the couch into our Papa's loving arms and be at peace. We can breathe here, think here, rest here. And once we are really comfortable and at home, we can invite others in and minister to them from this place.

Exchanged for the Chamber of Shame: *Openness*

I picture this chamber as one made of crystal-clear glass. There is no hiding here—it's a showcase! The fruits of the Spirit are on display here, as are the victories we have won, the scars we have borne, our humanness and godliness woven together in a marvelously displayed tapestry. And this chamber is not made of shatterproof, bulletproof glass—no—it is breakable, to be sure. However, living within us is the One who is able to fix it if and whenever it should break. The beauty of this chamber is its vulnerability, its fragility, and its transparency.

Exchanged for the Chamber of Fear: *Adoption*

Our status as sons and daughters, the knowledge of our value, our preciousness, and the lavish love bestowed on us by our Father cannot suffer fear in their midst. Perfect love has cast it out. As a newborn baby can rest defenseless and satisfied in the arms of its loving parents, so can the fully adopted son or daughter rest in the arms of the Father. This is a chamber within a chamber … or like a chamber within a womb. There is no fear here.

Beloved brothers and sisters, welcome home. Welcome to the family. You are loved here. You belong here. Make yourselves comfortable and at home and embrace the favored role you were born to play.

THE FOUR CHAMBERS
of the **GRAFTED-IN** HEART:

fellowship

home

openness

adoption

EPILOGUE

As I type these words, it's been a solid two years since I began writing this book. I confess I did not become fully grafted in by the time I finished writing it, and it's likely you won't, either, just because you've finished reading. It's a process. In chapter 5, I said that for olive trees and adopted children, it generally seems to take about three years for those roots to go down deep. The three-year mark since I began my own journey is drawing near, and the path I've taken has had many ups and downs, twists and turns.

Recently, I checked myself into a thirty-day residential treatment clinic. The circumstances that provoked this radical decision were not as dire or as frightening as my nuclear meltdown in the bushes I described in the prologue. It was more that I had just *had it.* Had it with the inner turmoil. Had it with not feeling in control of my emotions and, at times, my behavior. I was done, and I wanted change. Remember when I said, *If you want to live a radically transformed life, you will have to prepare yourself to get a little radical*? It was time to put my money where my mouth was, and this decision was radical, all right.

As I sat in the backseat of my ride to the clinic, I stared out the window, not wanting to make small talk with the driver. Hot tears streamed down my face in time with the questions that raced through my brain. I wondered what level of "crazy" the people at this clinic were. I wondered what level I was. How panicked and trapped would I feel while I was there? And, most importantly, *Will this work? What if it doesn't?*

Those questions arose out of my fears and worries, but deep down I was certain that *this time* I would finally get the complete healing I've desperately sought. Isaiah 50:7 came to mind:

> Because the Sovereign LORD helps me, I will not be disgraced. Therefore have I set my face like flint, and I know I will not be put to shame. (NIV)

And so I pushed forward, eyes and heart absolutely fixed on the prize that lay ahead. Fifty hours a week (*fifty hours!*) I sifted through the wreckage of my life and sorted it out. Not only did I tear down strongholds and lies, but with the help of my therapist, I identified the five most powerful and destructive lies that had become my unhealthy core beliefs:

1. I am powerless.
2. No one hears me.
3. I hate who I am.
4. I am a failure.
5. There is something terribly wrong with me.

These seemingly simplistic lies took significant digging to uncover, and their discovery emerged from tracing back repeated patterns of negative thoughts and feelings that formed in response to trauma throughout my lifetime. Once we discovered them, they seemed so obvious I wondered how I hadn't recognized them up until now!

Then the process of replacing those powerful lies with powerful truths began. My therapist told me I had to write these truths down in my own words—*my own voice*—in a way that would be palatable and believable to me later on when I needed them. I also needed to find evidence of these truths in Scripture and write those down alongside the ones in my own words.

Just as there was real work involved in digging out the lies, it was real work learning how to actually get the truths to stick. It meant facing down shame, ugly thoughts, and anger. *So much anger.* I had to learn how to face it, address it, deal with it, and get rid of it. I burned lies I scrawled on scraps of paper, smashed plates inscribed with painful memories, held a mock funeral for my old self. All of this was done carefully, deliberately, and with the help of the Holy Spirit. And with the knowledge that if I chose to hold on to any of those things, I had only myself to blame.

I learned a lot about how our brains process trauma and undergo biological and chemical changes as a result of it. Even better, I learned how we can form new, healthy neural pathways with repeated exposure to truth, positivity, and goodness. Basically practicing the good stuff we are taught right there in the Bible. In fact, I heard professionals at the clinic refer to the Bible as a "decision-making manual." That's a perspective I have not ever considered before!

I can't stress how hard I worked at all of this—not striving, but completely committed and determined to do my part in reaching a place of healing and wholeness. It was kind of the psycho-spiritual equivalent to running a marathon. All the work I did prior to entering the clinic was the initial training, and now it was time to actually run that grueling course. The finish line was the healing of the major traumas in my life I hadn't been able to overcome. That was the goal. But the prize at the end was something even better:

I am now fully grafted in.

I can feel it. And it's a solid, secure, joyful assurance I've never, ever been able to grasp before.

I know who I am now.

I actually *like* who I am.

And I know to Whom I belong.

My grafted-in heart is full, and I experience the inner fellowship of the Father, Son, and Holy Spirit. I feel their love and their delight in me. That aching loneliness is gone. My heart is at rest (at last!) and has found its home. I am comfortable in my own skin and with who I am, because I've moved into my Father's house, and I know I belong there. I have learned how to be open and vulnerable while having good boundaries, and I realize some of my greatest strengths come to the surface when I share deeply from my heart. My fears aren't completely gone, but their power has diminished significantly and they no longer rule my life. I now understand and know—down deep in my core—what it means to be, what it feels like, and how to live my life as a real daughter of the Father.

Chosen. Adopted.

Grafted in.

ACKNOWLEDGMENTS

First and foremost, all thanks and glory to you, Father, for your love, teaching, and leading throughout the process of writing this book. Your presence was so close each time I sat down to write, that reading through the book again brings back sweet memories of you. It truly was something we did together, and I can't wait for us to do it again.

To my husband, Mark: my hero, my best friend, my biggest cheerleader in anything I decide to do. How can I ever thank you for all you pour into me? My life and my healing are living testimonies to your love.

To each of my children: Erik, Ariel, Noel, Victoria, Emilee, and Martin. You don't know the depths of love I have for you or how much you've taught me about love itself. There is nothing on this earth that I count more valuable or irreplaceable than you.

To my steadfast tribe of girlfriends: Rachel, Jody, Deb, Kirstin, Danielle, Torrie, Tori, Kimberly, Carmella, Jenna, Jeanne, Cat, Lore, and Yelafer. At times, you were the glue that held me together. You inspire me, and you've inspired my next book.

To Mercy By the Sea, for allowing me an oceanfront sanctuary space to pray, meditate, and write this book.

To Alecia and Anita, my coach and my therapist, whose skill and care helped me heal and break through to new levels of freedom and wholeness.

To Kerby and Janna, whose lifelong friendships I hold so dear. Thank you for adding your excellence to this book. You make me look good!

To my advance reader team: John, Bryan, Dan, Tim, Dave, Scott, Alecia, Kimberly, and Lisa. You guys rock! Thanks so much for taking on this project sight unseen and for providing much-needed feedback.

To Anna LeBaron, for emerging out of the Twitter woodwork to encourage me to go for it and then pointing the way.

And to CityChurch New Haven, for being a place for me to heal, to grow, and to worship.

END NOTES

Chapter 1:

1. Henri J. M. Nouwen, *The Return of the Prodigal Son* (New York: Doubleday, 1992), 37.

2. Sylvia Plath, *The Unabridged Journals of Sylvia Plath*, https://www.goodreads.com/quotes/178991-god-but-life-is-loneliness-despite-all-the-opiates-despite; accessed March 18, 2018.

3. J.R.R. Tolkien, *The Fellowship of the Ring* (New York: Houghton Mifflin, 1994), 167.

4. Jack Frost, *Spiritual Slavery to Spiritual Sonship* (Shippensburg, PA: Destiny Image, 2006), 25.

5. Carl Jung, https://www.goodreads.com/quotes/347602-shame-is-a-soul-eating-emotion; accessed March 18, 2018.

6. Sarah Micula, "Lent Day 24: Sin Destroys Our Sense of Responsibility," *The Salvation Army Central Women USA,* March 4, 2016, http://uscwomensministries.com/2016/03/lent-day-24-sin-destroys-our-sense-of-responsibility/, accessed March 28, 2018.

7. Yann Martel, *Life of Pi* (New York: Houghton Mifflin Harcourt, 2001), 93.

8. Henri Miller, *Black Spring* (New York: Grove Press, 1963), 126.

9. Henri Nouwen, *You Are the Beloved: Daily Meditations for Spiritual Living* (New York: Convergent, 2017), 12.

10. Mother Teresa, https://www.goodreads.com/quotes/71796-being-unwanted-unloved-uncared-for-forgotten-by-everybody-i-think; accessed March 18, 2018.

11. Chuck Palahniuk, *Survivor: A Novel* (New York: W.W. Norton and Co, 1999), 162.

Chapter 4:

1. R. A. Torrey, *The Person and the Work of the Holy Spirit* (New York: Cosimo, 2007), 35–36.

2. Neil Anderson, quoted in "Why We Don't Have to Listen to Satan" by Ney Bailey, *Starting With God Blog*, https://www.startingwithgod.com/struggles/do-not-listen/; accessed March 18, 2018.

3. N. T. Wright, *Simply Christian: Why Christianity Makes Sense* (New York: HarperCollins, 2006), 129.

4. Ken Graham, "Translation of Abba," October 2016, https://hermeneutics.stackexchange.com/questions/46/translation-of-abba-Αββα-אבא; accessed April 6, 2018.

Chapter 5:

1. Information gathered from the following sources: Joe Ray, "The Road Back to Tradition Begins With a Graft," *Eating The Motherland Blog*, March 12, 2007, http://www.joe-ray.com/motherland/year/2007/; accessed March 18, 2018. Lynn Doxon, "How Grafting Affects Olive Trees," *Homeguides | SFgate*, http://homeguides.sfgate.com/grafting-affects-olive-trees-56828.html; accessed June 11, 2018. Carolyn Csanyi, "How to Graft Wild Olive Trees," *Homeguides | SFgate*, http://homeguides.sfgate.com/graft-wild-olive-trees-87778.html; accessed June 10, 2018.

2. Bruce Cockburn, "Lovers in a Dangerous Time," *Stealing Fire*, A&M Records, 1984.

Chapter 7
1. Augustine di Hippo, *Confessions* (London: Penguin, 1961), 4.
2. Mike Bickle, "How to Break a Mental Stronghold," *Charisma Magazine Online*, August 1, 2013, https://www.charismamag.com/spirit/spiritual-growth/172-strongholds-of-the-mind; accessed March 18, 2018.
3. David Herring, "Evolving in the Presence of Fire," *NASA Earth Observatory*, October 1999, https://earthobservatory.nasa.gov/Features/BOREASFire/; accessed March 18, 2018.
4. Henri J. M. Nouwen, *The Inner Voice of Love* (New York: Doubleday, 1996), 30–31.
5. Elevation Worship, "Grace So Glorious," *Only King Forever*, Provident Music Group, 2014.

Chapter 8:
1. Dietrich Bonhoeffer, *The Cost of Discipleship* (New York: Touchstone, 1995), 164.
2. Brené Brown, "The Power of Vulnerability," TEDxHouston, June 2010, https://www.ted.com/talks/brene_brown_on_vulnerability; accessed March 18, 2018.

Chapter 9:
1. Nelson Mandela, https://www.brainyquote.com/quotes/nelson_mandela_178789; accessed March 18, 2018.

2. Brené Brown, "The Power of Vulnerability Course," *Sounds True*, https://www.soundstrue.com/store/the-power-of-vulnerability-2917.html; accessed March 18, 2018.

3. Ibid.

4. Iskander Krayenbosch, "The Hero's Journey," *Vimeo*, 2015, https://vimeo.com/140767141; accessed March 18, 2018.

Chapter 10:

1. Henri J. M. Nouwen, excerpt from *Devotional Classics*, edited by Richard Foster and James Bryan Smith (San Francisco: Harper, 1993), 80.

2. John Arnott, *The Father's Blessing* (Lake Mary, Florida: Charisma House, 1995), 132.

3. Jamie Lee Curtis, *Tell Me Again About the Night I Was Born* (New York: HarperCollins, 2000).

4. John Eldridge, *EPIC: The Story God Is Telling* (Nashville: Thomas Nelson, 2004), 8.

5. CityWorship, "Home," *I Am Home*, CityWorship Records, 2016.

Chapter 11:

1. C. S. Lewis, *The Last Battle*: CHRONICLES OF NARNIA, BOOK SEVEN (New York: HarperCollins, 2002), 213.